Marriages of

BERTIE COUNTY, NORTH CAROLINA

1762-1868

Marriages of
BERTIE COUNTY,
NORTH CAROLINA

1762-1868

Compiled by
RAYMOND PARKER FOUTS

CLEARFIELD

Reprinted for
Clearfield Company, Inc. by
Genealogical Publishing Co., Inc.
Baltimore, Maryland
2005

NOTE

THE MARRIAGE RECORDS found herein were abstracted from the North Carolina Archives' microfilm series, *Bertie Marriage Bonds, 1762-1868* and *Bertie Marriage Register, 1851-1917.* The reader should note that marriage bonds provide evidence only of intent to marry and do not in themselves constitute proof of marriage. The original Bertie County marriage bonds are preserved in the Archives in Raleigh and cover the period from 1762 until 1851, when marriage licenses and certificates were required. Unless otherwise noted in this work, records dated prior to 1851 derive from marriage bonds. Licenses and certificates, along with some bonds, are preserved from 1851 on and show the actual date of the marriage. They were recorded in marriage register volumes maintained by the Register of Deeds in Windsor, North Carolina.

MARRIAGES OF BERTIE COUNTY, NORTH CAROLINA, 1762-1868

Abington, Littlebery & Sarah Moore, 4 May 1790; Titus
Moore, Bm.

Acre, Henry & Mary Ives, 29 Mar. 1793.

Acre, William & Elizabeth Mann, married 28 Jan. 1866.

Acree, John & Mary Brown, 9 Dec. 1800; Jno. Norfleet, Bm.

Acree, Leonard & Margaret Seay (?), 4 Oct. 1792; Micajah
(X) Wilkes, Bm.

Acree, Thomas & Elizabeth Higgs, 1 Mar. 1802; Lewis
Cotten, Bm.

Acree, William & Phereby Skinner, 12 Mar. 1791; Micajah
(X) Wilkes, Bm.

Adams, Elijah (X) & Judeth Roundtree, 29 Mar. 1793; Henry
Churchwell, Bm.

Adams, Robert (X) & Elisabeth Spivey, 5 Mar. 1785; Bryan
Smith, Bm.

Adams, W. A. & Frances Williams, married 1 July 1858.

Adams, William & Mary Ann Farless, married 6 Feb. 1868.

Adams, Wm. S. & Martha E. White, married 12 May 1862.

Adkin, Napoleon & Louiza Wilford, 11 Feb. 1850; James
Williford, Bm.

Adkinson, John & Joanna Matthews, married 22 Apr. 1858.

Alaxander, Robert G. & Victoria R. Outlaw, married 29 Dec.
1868.

Alexander, Thomas & Patricia C. Miller, married 11 June
1861; Josiah Miller, I. W. Miller, wit.

Allen, George & Winnefred Sowell, 10 June 1805; Ezekiel
Sowell, Bm.; Thos. Spence, wit.

1

Allen, Thomas & Janie Outlaw, married 25 June 1861 by
Cyrus Waters, Rector of St. Thomas Church, Windsor.

Allensworth, Nehemiah (X) & Cloe Morris, 29 Apr. 1783;
William (X) Cobb, Bm.; Stephen Outterbridge, James
Long, wit.

Alston, Jas. & Sarah White, married 8 Aug. 1860.

Alston, James & Ann E. Burden, married 27 Apr. 1865.

Alston, Norman & Sallie E. Watson, married 7 Apr. 1858 by
Benjn. S. Bronson, Rector of St. Thomas Church, Windsor.

Anderson, William & Jannett Marde, 18 Oct. 1808; Thos.
West, Bm.

Andrews, Britton & Winnefred Outlaw, 14 Feb. 1854; Eason
Ward, Bm. Married 16 Feb. 1854.

Andrews, George & Mary D. Acre, married 12 Dec. 1855.

Andrews, John & Winney Smith, 29 Oct. 1779; Charles Rhoads,
Bm.

Andrews, John L. & Celia J. Askew, 5 Jan. 1855 (lic.).
Married 10 Jan. 1855.

Appling, William & _____Barber, 21 June 1789; Richard
Swinson, Bm.

Armistead, Henry (Col.) & Martha Webb (Col.), 28 Dec. 1867
(lic.). Married 3 Jan. 1868; David Higgins, J. N. Webb,
Robbart Webb, wit.

Armistead, Robert & Sarah Jordan, 11 May 1782; William
Armistead, Bm.

Asbell, Alonzo (X) & Christian Farmer, 15 Nov. 1851.

Ashburn, John & Fanny Nicholls, 13 Feb. 1797; William
West Billups, Bm.

Ashburn, William & Frances Rasor, 11 May 1774; Edwd.___,
Thos. Shehan, Bm.

Askew, Aaron & Martha Alexander, 7 May 1805; Joshua
Outlaw, Bm.

Askew, David C. & Levina A. Jones, married 20 Dec. 1860.

Askew, Elpsy & Nancy Futrell, married 30 Mar. 1866.

Askew, Garrisson & Pricilla Harrel, 8 Oct. 1850; John (X)
Askew, Bm.

BERTIE MARRIAGES, 1762-1868

Askew, J. A. J. & Mariah Holder, 16 Aug. 1853; H. H. White,
Bm. Married 18 Aug. 1853.

Askew, John & Mary Duning, 17 Aug. 1790; Charles Duning,
Bm.

Askew, John & Mary Outlaw, 2 Jan. 1793; William Spivey, Bm.

Askew, Josiah & Mary Outlaw, 12 Feb. 1796; William Watford,
Bm.

Askew, Thos. R. & Ann Eliza Gill, 22 Dec. 1851; Wilie
Askew, Bm.

Askew, Watson & Ellen White, married 14 July 1866.

Askew, William J. (of Hertford Co.) & Nancy Adaline
Sessoms, married 2 May 1854.

Askew, Wm. LaFayette & Mary E. Sharrack, married 7 May
1863.

Askew, William W. & Celia Eason, married 27 Feb. 1862;
Thomas Mitchell, Joseph Ruffin, John Mitchell, wit.

Askew, Willie & Mary W. Gill, 3 Nov. 1857 (lic.). Married
22 (?) Nov. 1857.

Atkinson, Jordan (X) & Martha Roberson, 13 May 1799; Henry
Blackson, Bm.

Averet, Henry & Elizabeth Abbington, 7 Oct. 1777; Hardyman
Abington, Bm.

Averet, Henry & Sarah Montgomery, 9 May 1792; Joseph Moore,
Bm.

Averet, James & Sarah Powell, 23 Dec. 1786; James Powell,
Bm.

Avrit, Alexander & Mary Raybey, 31 Aug. 1778; John Dodrill,
Bm.

Ayers, Robert & Francis Denty, 21 Aug. 1854 (lic.). Married
22 Aug. 1854.

Azbell, Solomon (X) & Sarah Jernigan, 25 Aug. 1784; James
Sowell, Bm.

Bailey, Maga (Major?) William (X) & Rhodea Yates, 30 June
1792; William Griffen, Bm.

Bailey, Willis & Salley Rhodes, 14 Aug. 1802; Moses
Gillam, Bm.

3

BERTIE MARRIAGES, 1762-1868

Baker, David & Polly Jernigan, 17 Jan. 1828; Lewis (X)
Jernegan, Bm.

Baker, Elias (X) & Elizabeth Harrell, 2 Aug. 1785; Peter
(X) Evans, Bm.

Baker, George W. & Martha S. Coffield, 6 Sept. 1866 (lic.).
Married 12 Sept. 1866.

Baker, Henry & Martha Cale, 3 Mar. 1840; Wm. S. Pruden,
Bm.

Baker, Isaac & Mary Outlaw, 26 Dec. 1807; John Wynns, Bm.

Baker, Jeremiah (X) & Elizabeth Curry, 22 Sept. 1808;
William Coffield, Bm.; B. Ashburn, wit.

Baker, John & Martha Cherry, 17 Sept. 1790; William
Standley, Bm.

Baker, John (X) & Penelope Brown, 9 Jan. 1854 (lic.).
Married 10 Jan. 1854.

Baker, John & Mary Baker, 25 Feb. 1854; Richard (X) Parker,
Bm. Married 19 Feb. 1854 (sic); Charles T. Jenkins, James
Williford, Asa Williford, wit.

Baker, John Wright & Mary Jane Flood, married 15 Oct. 1859.

Baker, Levi (X) & Polley Williford, 24 Aug. 1803; John
Early, Bm.

Baker, Levy (X) & Polly Churchwell, 5 June 1806; W. Veale,
Bm.

Baker, Richard & Betsey Baker, 22 June 1787; John Moore, Bm.

Baker, Richard & Nelly Ann Miller, married 3 Aug. 1859.

Baker, Samuel & Lizzy Baker, 18 Sept. 1820; Jesse (X) Wood,
Bm.

Baker, William (X) & Polly Bowen, 7 Dec. 1805; Henry (X)
Cobb, Bm.; Thos. Spence, wit.

Baker, William W. (X) & Peggy Jacobs, 16 Aug. 1799;
Jonathan (X) Harman, Bm.

Baker, William Wilson (X) & Fereby Jobe (?), 24 Aug. 1795;
John Douglas, Bm.

Ballance, James M. & Wiley Ann Smith, married 4 Jan. 1860.

Baradill, James & Sarah Standley, 26 Feb. 1793; David
Spivey, Bm.

4

Barber, Charles (X) & Prudence Castalaw, 1 July 1774;
Hugh Hyman, Bm.

Barber, Charles (X) & Elizabeth Bentley, 12 Apr. 1780;
Epaphras Moore, Bm.

Barber, Cullen & Anny Clifton, 19 May 1800; Luke Warburton,
Bm.

Barber, Frederick & Mary Bentley, 25 Oct. 1803; William
D. Barber, Bm.

Barber, William D. & Nancy Griffen, 2 Aug. 1803; Miles
Bonner, Bm.

Barbour, Charles & Mary A. Harris, 9 Sept. 1850; John
R. McGlauhon, Bm.

Barksdale, William & Christen Sumner, 7 Apr. 1788; Henry
Hill, Bm.

Barnacastle, Beverley (X) & Fanny Knott, 9 Dec. 1797;
Nathan (X) Bowin, Bm.

Barnacastle, Charles & Sally Byram, 7 July 1853; Levi
Harden, Bm. Married 8 July 1853.

Barnacastle, Kenneth & Wm. Emily Baley, married 11 Feb.
1867.

Barnacastle, Samuel & Matilda Jones, 19 July 1824;
Beverly (X) Barnacastle, Bm.

Barnacastle, Wm. R. & Mary M. Phelps, married 11 Mar. 1868.

Barnes, Reuben (X) & Nancy Martin, 16 July 1802; Jesse
Raser, Bm.

Barnes, Richard & Elizabeth Veale, married 11 Dec. 1856.

Barnes, Richard H. & Georgeanna Cox, 5 Sept. 1853; John
H. Acree, Bm. Married 8 Sept. 1853.

Barnhill, Blount & Clara Rhodes, married 21 Jan. 1867.

Barns, Asa & Margaret Casper, married 4 Oct. 1854; William
Cooper, Anderson Casper, wit.

Barns, Cader (X) & Elizabeth Wimberley, 3 Jan. 1786;
Thomas (X) Griffin, Jas. (X) Wilford, Bm.

Barns, James & Elisabeth Cook, 13 Apr. 1799; William (X)
Cook, Bm.

Barrett, J. W. & Penelope White, Married 16 Oct. 1866.

BERTIE MARRIAGES, 1762-1868

Bartley, Henry & Edith Butler, 1 June 1804; William W. Johnston, Bm.; Kenneth Clark, wit.

Basman, John & Mary Weston, 22 Dec. 1789; John Weston, Bm.

Bass, Alpheus & Mary F. Morris, 10 June 1865 (lic.). Married 15 June 1865.

Bass, Augustus & Martha Morris, married 17 Jan. 1861.

Bass, Benjamin H. & Ann Clifton, 22 Dec. 1828.

Bass, Council (X) & Patty Griffin, 4 May 1782; Cader Bass, Bm.

Bass, Jacob & Mary Lassiter, 8 Sept. 1789; Israel Outhouse, Bm.

Bass, John & Nancey Penney, 26 May 1797; Isom Wilford, Bm.

Bass, Thomas & Martha Britt, married 14 Nov. 1854.

Bateman, George & Lurany Gardner, 2 June 1807; Luke Smithwick, Bm.

Bayly, Thomas & Elizabeth M. Lawrence, married 23 Dec. 1856.

Bazemore, Abisha & Amelia Mizells, 11 Aug. 1853; John W. Laciter, Bm. Married 11 Aug. 1853.

Bazemore, Armstead L. & Celia E. Cherry, 6 June 1865 (lic.). Married 6 June 1865.

Bazemore, Edward & Celia Peele, 19 Apr. 1851; Thomas Cherry, Bm. Married 22 Apr. 1851; Allen Bazemore, Henry Bazemore, wit.

Bazemore, Hezekiah & Lydia Brayboy, 26 Feb. 1805; Elisha Bazemore, Bm.

Bazemore, Joseph P. & Drucilla Bazemore, married 20 Dec. 1860.

Bazemore, Kenneth & Mary Butler, 15 Dec. 1852; Wm. J. (X) Copeland, Bm. Married 21 Dec. 1852; Wm. T. Chapel, John Copeland, wit.

Bazemore, Peyton & Penelope Johnston, 20 Feb. 1828; Jos. Thomas, Bm.

Bazemore, Reddin & Hannah Thomas, 11 Apr. 1831; Mikel Thomas, Bm.

Bazemore, Reddin & Jane Taylor, married 14 Apr. 1857.

6

Bazemore, Sampson & Emilina Lee, married 24 Feb. 1867.

Bazemore, Thomas H. & Ann M. Bazemore, 12 Oct. 186_ (lic.). Married 14 Oct. 1863.

Bazemore, Wm. H. & Martha A. Parker, married 6 Jan. 1859.

Bazemore, Wm. J. & Mary E. Bazemore, married 5 Jan. 1860.

Bazemore, Willis & Martha Ann Lee (Col.), married 27 May 1866; John J. Gardner, Bryant Lee (Col.), wit.

Bazmore, Abisha & Heziah Chapel, 17 May 1806; Jesse Bazemore, Jr., Bm.

Bazmore, Elisha & Annis Wilford, 29 June 1804; Wm. Sowell, Bm.

Bazmore, James (X) & Mary Thompson, 16 Feb. 1808; Abisha Bazmore, Bm.

Bazmore, Jesse & Penelope Basemore, 26 Jan. 1799; James (X) Wilford, Bm.

Bazmore, Stephen & Polly Bynum, 12 Nov. 1799; Phillip Stallings, Bm.

Beasley, George & Edy Hardy, married 22 Sept. 1866.

Beasley, Thos. & Acenith Heckstall, 13 Dec. 1849; J. L. Britton, Jona. S. Tayloe, Bm.

Beasly, Noah & Celia Perry, married __ Jan. 1867.

Bell, Benja. & Absila Norflet, 2 July 1768; Arthur Brown, Bm.

Bell, Bright & Mourning Cobb, 22 Feb. 1800; Henry Cobb, Bm.

Belote, Henry (X) & Elisabeth Bentley, 9 ___ 1782; Nottingham Monk, Bm.

Belote, John & Elisabeth Stallings, 8 Jan. 1785; Noah Belote, Bm.

Belote, Peleg (X) & Eliza. Edwards, 9 June 1786; James (X) Ward, Bm.

Belote, Thomas & Ann North, 21 Feb. 1798; James Stuart, Bm.

Benbury, John A. & Harriet A. Ryan, married 23 June 1859.

Bentley, James & Elizabeth Bird, 7 Feb. 1795; Solomon Nobles, Bm.; Andrew Bittle, wit.

Bentley, Jeremiah & Margaret Maning, 4 Feb. 1800; Charney Curl, Bm.

Bentley, John & Pressila Manning, 23 Nov. 1779; William Hyman, Bm.

Bentley, John (X) & Anne Hardy, 17 Aug. 1792; James Ross, Bm.

Bentley, John & Mary Lawrence, 30 Aug. 1796; Luke Manning, Bm.

Bernard, S. A. & Winafred E. Gillam, 20 Jan. 1848.

Berry, Eason (Col.) & Esther Gilbert (Col.), 31 Aug. 1867 (lic.). Married 1 Feb. 1868.

Berry, Richard (X) & Elisabeth Acree, 1 Mar. 1802; Thomas Acree, Bm.

Berry, Wright & Sarah Ward, 21 Jan. 1782; Samuel (X) Haste, Bm.

Best, Henry & Milley Morriss, 17 Jan. 1789; John Moriss, Bm.

Best, Thomas & Winefred Wood, 24 Dec. 1790; William Morriss, Bm.

Biggs, Simon & Amy Thompson, married __ Jan. 1867.

Billups, John & Sarah Bonner, 19 Dec. 1772; John White, Bm.

Billups, Thomas & Sarah Mohn, 17 Feb. 1796; Eli Mohn, Bm.

Billups, William & Elizabeth Fleetwood, 23 May 1787; Robert West, Bm.

Binkley, Eli & Salley Gaskins, 26 Nov. 1788; James Hardy, Bm.

Birch, James & Martha Lasseter, married 2 Nov. 1854.

Bird, Edward & Elizabeth Razer, 15 May 1762; Jasper Hardison, Frederick Bell, Bm.

Bird, Godwin & Nancy Jane Valentine, 3 Mar. 1858 (lic.). Married 4 Mar. 1858.

Bird, Godwin & Mary E. Brown, married 24 Jan. 1861.

Bird, Henry & Caroline Castello, married 27 Aug. 1854; Benj. Miller, wit.

BERTIE MARRIAGES, 1762-1868

Bird, Jackson & Mary Boswell, 27 Apr. 1851; William (X)
Bird, Bm. Married 27 Apr. 1851; Will. C. Miller, John
Butler, Augustus Holder, wit.

Bird, James & Emily Miller, 24 June 1854 (lic.). Married
25 June 1854.

Bird, James & Emiline Butler, married 3 June 1866; Robert
Brown, William Folk, wit.

Bird, John (X) & Louay Jernigan, 26 June 1805; James Keen,
Bm.

Bird, Joseph B. & Margaret Williams, married 27 May 1866.

Bird, Richard & Clarissa Butler, 13 Aug. 1827; Wm. H.
Green, Bm.

Bird, William (X) & Margaret Boswell, 13 Apr. 1853. Married 14 Apr. 1853; Ryan Butler, Thaddeous H. Butler, wit.

Bird, William W. & Rutha Cobb, married 10 Apr. 1859.

Bird, William Watson & Friza Perry, married 31 May 1866.

Bishop, Erastus R. & Susan L. Worley, 20 Dec. 1853 (lic.).
Married 20 Dec. 1853.

Bishop, Gipson & Nancy Bishop, married 8 Apr. 1866.

Bishop, Jacob & Mary Tyler, married 8 Apr. 1866.

Bishop, Joshua & Venus Bishop, married 8 Apr. 1866.

Bishop, William & Mary Horn, 29 Sept. 1827; Thos. Ruffin,
Bm.; Thomas P. Slade, wit.

Bittle, John & Polly Cole, 29 Mar. 1798; Andrew Bittle, Bm.

Bizzel, Elisha & Betsey Love, 22 May 1828.

Black, Samuel & Elizabeth Hardey, 10 Oct. 1765; Robert
West, Bm.

Blackston, John F. & Milissa Ann Burket, married 6 Nov.
1860.

Blanchard, Miles & Sarah Hyman, 19 Apr. 1787; Amos Rayner,.
Wm. (X) Rawls, Bm.

Blaxton, Thos. H. & Elizabeth Boyce, 10 Dec. 1824; Jona.
S. Tayloe, Bm.

Blount, Benj. B. & Elizabeth Godwine, 5 Apr. 1827; Matthias
B. D. Palmer, Bm.

Blount, Calvin & Susan Holliday, married 19 May 1859.

Blount, Jesse (X) & Rebecha Bartlet, 28 Feb. 1788; Jesse (X) Cooper, Bm.

Blount, John & Elizabeth Milburn, 13 Jan. 1790; Wyrriott Blount, Bm.

Blount, Stevens & Prudence Holley, 19 Sept. 1798; John L. Blount, Bm.

Bond, Dave & Patty Bond, married 6 Aug. 1866.

Bond, George & Mary Rhodes, 25 Sept. 1806; John Ruffin, Bm.

Bond, James & Sarah W. Bond, married 25 Nov. 1856 by Benj. S. Bronson, Rector of St. Thomas Church, Windsor.

Bond, John & (Mrs.) Anna Smith, 5 Feb. 1784; Wm. Gray, Bm.

Bond, John & Sarah West, 15 Dec. 1797; K. T. Strother, Bm.

Bond, John (Col.) & Sally Bond (Col.), 9 Nov. 1867 (lic.). Married 9 Nov. 1867.

Bond, Lewis & Hannah Dawson, 29 Oct. 1799; Jason Gardner, Bm.

Bond, Lewis & Annie H. Carter, 1 Dec. 18__; H. Nicholls, Bm. Married 4 Dec. 1851.

Bond, Thomas & Edey House, 14 Oct. 1780; Wm. Gray, Bm.

Bond, Thomas & Rhodea Bond, 30 Dec. 1790; Stevens Gray, Bm.; D. Strachan, wit.

Bond, Thomas & Tempey Leggett, 28 May 1806; Wm. Lee Gray, Bm.

Bonner, Thomas & Elisabeth Dugin, 4 May 1802; Miles Bonner, Bm.

Boon, Joseph (X) & Mary Boon, 17 Dec. 1779; John (X) Low, Bm.

Boswell, Charles & Margaret Saward, 7 Oct. 1790; Ransom Billups, Bm.

Boswell, Edward & Selah Todd, 1 Jan. 1810; Thos. Boswell, Bm.

Boswell, Edward & Penelope Bazemore, married 18 Jan. 1866.

Boswell, Thomas & Maria Henry, married 17 Nov. 1867.

Boswell, William (X) & Susanah Holder, 19 Apr. 1797;
Elisha Holder, Bm.

Bowen, Cornelius & Charlotte Todd, 2 May 1827; Jesse Bowen,
Bm.

Bowen, Edward & Harriet Myers, 21 Aug. 1828; Joshua Bowen,
Bm.

Bowen, Hardy & Penelope Cobb, 3 Jan. 1787; Benjamin (X)
Bowen, Abner Lawrence, Bm.; John Slade, wit.

Bowen, Holloway E. & Francis A. White, 18 Oct. 1853;
Cornelius Bowen, Bm. Married 18 Oct. 1853.

Bowen, Humphrey H. & Margaret Winnifred Bowen, 19 Dec.
1854 (lic.). Married 21 Dec. 1855.(sic)

Bowen, Humphry H. & Frances Ann Leicester, 3 Jan. 1859
(lic.). Married 4 Jan. 1859.

Bowen, James Hardy & Mary Williams, 22 Nov. 1854 (lic.).
Married 23 Nov. 1854.

Bowen, Jesse & Margt. Gregory, 25 Apr. 1833; William C.
Bird, Bm.

Bowen, John (X) & Winefred Speights, 16 Mar. 1801; Abner
Lawrence, Bm.

Bowen, Joshua (X) & Margaret Cobb, 27 July 1801; Elisha
(X) Corbert, Bm.

Bowen, Nathan & Martha Barnacastle, 29 Aug. 1797; John
Barrett, Bm.

Bowen, W. H. & Mary W. Butterton, married 12 July 1860.

Bowen, Wm. E. & Francis M. Barnacastle, 10 Dec. 1857 (lic.).
Married 13 Dec. 1857.

Bowin, F. C. & Elizabeth Pierce, 26 Aug. 1865 (lic.).
Married 7 Sept. 1865.

Boyce, Christopher (X) & Anny Hoggard, 9 Mar. 1802; Zadock
Mitchell, Bm.

Boyce, David (X) & Susanna Mitchel, 9 Nov. 1792; John (X)
Boyce, Bm.

Boyce, Hardy & Mary Hubbord, 13 Aug. 1790; Drury Melone, Bm.

Boyce, Hardy & Nancy Sholar, 30 Oct. 1801; Saml. W. Johnston,
Bm.

Boyce, William (X) & Judeth Lamb, 3 May 1787; Henry (X)
Belote, Bm.

Branch, Bolden P. & Mary F. Peele, married 27 Nov. 1859.

Branch, Burwell & Nancy Morgan, 15 Oct. 1788; Garrord
Wair, Bm.

Branch, John & Mary E. Bond, 9 Nov. 1853; Alfred Jones,
Bm. Married 9 Nov. 1853.

Brantly, Edwd. & Clarissa Cale, 10 May 1832; Zach. Ellissun,
Bm.

Brayboy, John (X) & Sarah Thomas, 26 Nov. 1800; John (X)
Thomas, Bm.

Brewer, Louis T. & Henrietta V. Cox, 8 Sept. 1866 (lic.).
Married 15 Sept. 1866.

Bridger, Robert & Margaret Mongomery, 2 Nov. 1786.

Bridger, Robert M. & Hannah E. Bazemore, 11 July 1853 (lic.).
Married 12 July 1853.

Briggs, Francis N. & Martha W. Hancock, married 6 Nov. 1856.

Britain, Daniel & Sarah Outlaw, 3 May 1803; Lewis Outlaw,
Bm.

Britt, Benjamen & Celia Wilford, 26 Dec. 1808; Henry Peteman,
Bm.

Britt, H. J. & Elizabeth Oxley, 11 Jan. 1848.

Britt, Jesse (X) & Sarah Cook, 30 July 1793; Thomas Harden,
Bm.; David Yeats, wit.

Britt, Josiah & Priscilla Floyd, 1 Feb. 1797; John Moore,
Bm.; Geo. Outlaw, wit.

Britt, Thomas & Martha King, 2 Mar. 1793; Michael King, Bm.

Britton, John C. & Mollie J. Simons, married 6 Dec. 1868.

Britton, Richd. A. & Margt. E. Spivey, 10 Nov. 1830; Joseph
D. White, Bm.

Brogdon, Aaron (X) & Sarah Brogdon, 21 Dec. 1802; Thomas
(X) Brogdon, Bm.

Brogdon, David (X) & Susanah Mackhenry, 13 Dec. 1786; John
Brogdon, Bm.

Brogdon, Edward & Volley Blount, 9 Dec. 1805; Jonathan Skiles,
Bm.

Brogdon, John (X) & Susanna Hogard, 12 Oct. 1785; John (X) Skiles, Bm.

Brogdon, Thos. (X) & Sarah Jones, 4 Jan. 1794; William (X) Brogdon, Bm.; Willm. Burlingham, wit.

Brogdon, Thomas (X) & Thamer Skiles, 9 Feb. 1796; Soln. Cherry, Bm.

Brogdon, Timothy & Sarah McHenry, 18 Aug. 1791; Thomas (X) Brogdon, Bm.

Broglin, William & Mary Ann Rawls, married 22 Nov. 1866.

Brooks, Dunnen (X) & Apraley Standley, 20 Apr. 1804; Elisha (X) Cook, Bm.

Brooks, James & Luvina Hassel, 16 July 1851 (lic.). Married 17 July 1851.

Brown, A. J. & Sarah Williams, married 11 Feb. 1866.

Brown, D. G. L. P. & (Mrs.) Mary O. Shields, married 6 Feb. 1868.

Brown, Elisha & Sally Francis Robertson, 27 Nov. 1861 (lic.). Married 28 Nov. 1861.

Brown, Jackson & Basha Perry, 20 Jan. 1866 (lic.). Married 21 Jan. 1866.

Brown, John & Tempy Harrell, 12 Aug. 1794; William Higgs, Bm.

Brown, Joseph (X) & Happy Wood, 27 Jan. 1787; William Wood, Bm.

Brown, Lewis & Marinna Clark, married 8 May 1866.

Brown, Robert & Penece Early, 28 Aug. 1852; John (X) Ray, Bm.; P. H. Winston, wit. Married 2 Sept. 1852.

Brown, Robert & Henrietta Holder, married 23 May 1867.

Brown, Rowan (X) & Celia Peele, 5 Mar. 1821; Hary Phelps, Bm.

Brown, Ruffin (Col.) & Milly Hill (Col.), 26 Apr. 1867 (lic.). Married 11 May 1867.

Brown, Starkey & Priscilla Belch, 26 Mar. 1857 (lic.). Married 31 Mar. 1857.

Brown, Stephen D. & Lucy Carr, 23 Dec. 1850; Thos. E. Fanning, Bm.

13

BERTIE MARRIAGES, 1762-1868

Brown, William & Debby Stone, 21 Feb. 1795; Solomon Miller, Bm.

Brown, William & Martha Bird, married 5 Feb. 1863.

Bruce, Cader (X) & Sally Howard, 28 Dec. 1808; Axum Duns-more, Bm.

Bruce, Robert & Elizabeth Wynns, 8 Nov. 1852; Andrew J. Askew, Bm.

Bryan, Frederick & Amelia Pugh, 14 Feb. 1780; Jesse Averit, Bm.

Bryan, Harrison & Martha Jane Cox, 1 Feb. 1859 (lic.). Married 3 Feb. 1859.

Bryan, John & Ruth Sholar, 20 Feb. 1787; John Harrell, Bm.

Bryan, Joseph & Pheriby Smith, 26 Mar. 1766; William Alston, Bm.; John Johnston, wit.

Bryan, Joseph & Mary Dawson (widow), 11 Aug. 1774; William Bryan, Bm.

Bryan, Joseph & Elizabeth Cale, married 2 June 1857.

Bryant, James & Anna E. Rayner, 8 Jan. 1851; W. A. Ferguson, Bm.

Bryant, Joseph & Francis Mitchell, married 31 Oct. 1855.

Bryant, Martin & Ada Jones, 7 June 1853; James Magee, Bm. Married 12 June 1853.

Bryant, Wm. A. & Aletha Peel, 20 Feb. 1850; R. H. Cox, Bm.

Buck, Stephen & Elizabeth Cobb, 1 Nov. 1778; Andrew South, Bm.

Bunch, Henry & Ellenor Boysson, 29 Feb. 1764; Embrey Bunch, Thos. (X) Bass, Bm.

Bunch, Jesse H. & Barbara Ward, married 4 July 1866.

Bunch, John A. (of Chowan Co.) & Ann R. Gaskins, married 2 Dec. 1858.

Bunch, John D. & Sarah Jane Peele, married 17 Jan. 1867.

Bunch, Jos. W. & Lydia Baccus, married 26 Dec. 1868.

Bunch, Micajah & Levina Holder, 8 Apr. 1791; Elisha Holder, Bm.

BERTIE MARRIAGES, 1762-1868

Bunch, Micajah (X) & Edy Holder, 22 Feb. 1797; Jeremiah
Bunch, Bm.

Bunch, Micajah & Teletha Smith, 17 Nov. 1801; Micajah (X)
Bunch, Bm.

Bunch, Nehemiah J. & Elizabeth Jane Basemore, 31 Mar. 1853;
Robert M. Bridger, Bm. Married 31 Mar. 1853.

Bunch, William & Mary Bunch, 23 Dec. 1785; Frederick Bunch,
Bm.

Bunch, William & _____ Butler, married 4 June 1861.

Burdan, Bryant & Harriet Mitchell, married 4 July 1866.

Burdan, James & Mary E. Cherry, married 27 Sept. 1860.

Burden, James M. & Celia F. Dunning, married 2 Nov. 1865.

Burden, William (X) & Phebe Mitchel, 22 Sept. 1795; Jonathan Spivey, Bm.

Burden, William G. & Sarah E. Spivey, married 29 Sept. 1868.

Burden, Zadock Jackson & Emilla Jane Peele, 28 Dec. 1853.
Married 29 Dec. 1853.

Burket, William (X) & Phereby Jackson, 6 Aug. 1792; William Watson, Bm.

Burket, William (X) & Celia Johnston, 1 July 1797; John
Standley, Bm.

Burn, James & Sarah Howe, 27 Oct. 1784; Wm. Gray, Bm.

Burress, William & Belinda Taylor, married 17 Jan. 1866.

Burros, Daniel & Elisabeth Lawrence, 6 Jan. 1801; William
(X) Williams, Bm.

Bush, James & Sarah Walton, married 27 June 1859.

Butler, Benjamin & Mary Cole, married 27 Aug. 1863.

Butler, Curre & Elizabeth Phulks, 12 Jan. 1793; James
Hardy, Thomas Castellaw, Bm.

Butler, Harvey & Martha Jernigan, 28 Nov. 1857 (lic.).
Married 29 Nov. 1857.

Butler, Jacob J. & E. J. Bunch, married 28 June 1866.

Butler, Jethro (X) & Winefred Tiner, 16 Aug. 1791; Joseph
Mitchel, Bm.

15

Butler, John (X) & Mary Hubbard, 13 Feb. 1802; Reuben
Harrisson, Bm.

Butler, Jno. & Polly Dundalow, 18 Feb. 1850; Johnson Cow-
and, Bm.

Butler, John T. & Jane Adams, married 10 Jan. 1860.

Butler, John Thomas & Caroline Price, married 11 Apr. 1857.

Butler, Kader & Mary E. Davidson, 26 May 1857 (lic.).
Married 27 May 1857.

Butler, Kenneth & Harriette Pritchard, 19 Mar. 1853; Worley (X) Butler, Bm. Married 20 Mar. 1853.

Butler, Kenneth & Louisanna Lane, married 26 Dec. 1855.

Butler, Leven & Harriet Muzells, 10 Mar. 1827; William (X)
Mitchell, Bm.

Butler, Lorenzo & Amanda Oxley, married 16 Jan. 1856.

Butler, Marcus & Caroline Brown, married 27 Dec. 1866;
Wm. H. Butler, James Bird, wit.

Butler, Ryan (X) & Betsey Boswell, 14 June 1828.

Butler, Thadeus W. & Emily Dale, married 20 Dec. 1855;
John Irwin (?), wit.

Butler, William & Judah Hughes, 11 Feb. 1828; Wm. Watford,
Bm.

Butler, Wm. Hill & Eliza Jane Grant, married 22 Nov. 1866.

Butler, Williamston & Sarah Ward, married 24 June 1857.

Butler, Williamston & Margaret Philps, married 28 July 1861;
W. A. Fergason, George Hoggard, Joseph Mosre (?), wit.

Butler, Williamston & Sarah E. Stewart, married 21 Oct.
1862; William E. Bowen, Charles Mezill, wit.

Butter, Silas & Elizabeth Simons, 9 May 1808; George Simons,
Bm.

Butterton, Charles & Ann Stanton, 28 Sept. 1804; John Fleetwood, Bm.

Butterton, Charles & Elizabeth Thomas, 1 Jan. 1833; Willie
Griffin, Bm.

Butterton, James H. & Celia Bowen, married 18 Oct. 1860.

Buttery, Thomas F. & Jennet Canada, 18 Mar. 1842; Lewis Thomas, Bm.

Buttler, John (X) & Kezee Pritchard, 27 Dec. 1797; Christopher Pritchard, Bm.

Byram, Bellison (?) & Elizabeth Dempsey, married 17 Mar. 1866; Starkey E. Mizells, David H. Lawrence, wit.

Byram, George F. & Sallie J. Garrett, 20 Oct. 1865 (lic.). Married 25 Oct. 1865.

Byram, James & Sally Pugh, married 29 Nov. 1855.

Byram, James & Mary Pritchard, 1 Jan. 1859 (lic.). Married 6 Jan. 1859.

Byram, Jesse & Francis Jane Pierce, married 30 May. 1867.

Byram, Thomas & Martha Brown, married 20 Feb. 1868.

Byram, Thos. H. & Mary Frances "Fannie" Leicester, married 9 Nov. 1865.

Byrd, Richard (X) & Elisabeth Sparkman (dau. of Edward Sparkman), 30 July 1785; George (X) Sparkman, Bm.

Byrim, William & Nancy Page, 30 Aug. 1827; James (X) Tucker, Bm.

Byrum, Abner (X) & Milley Cooper, __Aug. 1790; Isack (X) Wilson, Bm.; Drury Melone, wit.

Byrum, David (X) & Elizabeth Wilson, 27 Apr. 1795; James Jernigan, Bm.

Byrum, Ira & Kizzy Barnes, 4 Jan. 1831; George Holloman, Bm.

Byrum, James & Milley Keen, 16 Aug. 1791; Joshua (X) Cherry, Bm.

Byrum, William (X) & Nancy Basemore, 18 Aug. 1798; Stephen Bazemore, Bm.

Cail, William (X) & Luckey Brogdon, 10 Aug. 1796; David Canaday, Bm.

Cale, Charney (X) & Elizabeth Harmon, 24 Oct. 1804; James (X) Wood, Bm.

Cale, Charney, Jr. & Kiddy Mizell, 8 Dec. 1849; Charney Cale, Bm.

Cale, Eason & Ann Mary White, 4 Dec. 1850; David (X) Pierce, Bm.

Cale, T. F. & May A. Outlaw, married 15 Sept. 1866.

Cale, William (X) & Sarah Mitchell, 16 May 1806; Christopher
Fig, Bm.

Cale, Wm. R. & (Mrs.) Mary Cale, married 1 Dec. 1868.

Calloway, John & Ann Temples, 21 June 1827; Samuel South,
Bm.

Campbell, Jono. & Celia Freeman, 23 Mar. 1793; Stevens
Gray, Bm.; Geo. Outlaw, wit.

Canady, James & Patsey Bentley, 25 Sept. 1799; Hum. R.
Smithwick, Bm.

Cannady, David & Ann Byrum, 12 Feb. 1789; George Dawson,
John (X) Petty, Bm.

Capehart, B. A. & Meeta Armistead, 4 Dec. 1858 (lic.).
Married 13 Dec. 1858 at residence of Cullen Capehart, Esq.

Capehart, Cademus & Mary M. Capehart, married 28 Dec. 1868.

Capehart, Henry (Col.) & Hannah Heckstall (Col.), married
6 Mar. 1867.

Capehart, John & Martha Rasor, 5 Aug. 1796; John Hardy, Bm.

Capehart, John & Nancy Cobb, 5 Feb. 1806; Henry (X) Cobb, Bm.

Capehart, John M. & Pauline A. Capehart, 8 Aug. 1849; Jona.
S. Tayloe, Bm.

Capehart, Michael & Sarah Butterton, 4 Apr. 1796; Curre
Butler, Bm.

Capehart, Richard Robert & Patsey Cobb, 24 Dec. 1852;
Calvin Hogwood, Bm. Married 26 Dec. 1852.

Capehart, Thomas & Mary Carter, 30 Jan. 1799; Josiah Rasor,
Bm.

Capehart, Thos. J. & Sally Ann Holloman, married 22 Jan.
1867.

Capehart, William & Mary Browne, 20 June 1798; Jonathan
Hardy, Bm.

Capehart, William A. & Annie M. Weston, married 7 Aug. 1867.

Capehart, William H. & Sarah E. Capehart, married 10 Oct.
1860.

Capps, John & Margaret Capehart, married 12 Mar. 1857.

Capps, John R. & Winnifred Ann Keeter, 20 Feb. 1860 (lic.).
Married 21 Feb. 1860.

Capps, John R. & Matilda Keeter, 4 Dec. 1865 (lic.). Married 5 Dec. 1865.

Caps, Moses (X) & Anne Rigsbey, 4 Aug. 1797; Josiah (X)
Rigsbey, Bm.

Carney, Josiah & Sarah Power, 19 Aug. 1789; Thomas Sutton,
Bm.

Carter, James (X) & Seasey Tarlington, 31 Dec. 1802; David
Combes, Bm.

Carter, Joseph & Catharine Belote, 21 Nov. 1786; John
Belote, Bm.

Carter, Lewis & Nancy Holloman, 27 June 1795; Abner Willeford, Bm.

Carter, Samuel (X) & Elisabeth Holly, 14 May 1779; William
Gray, Bm.

Carter, Thomas & Ailsey Mizells, 22 Aug. 1827; Elijah Rayner, Bm.

Carter, Turner (X) & Elitha Jenkens, 13 Oct. 1804; Francis
Pugh, Bm.

Carter, Wm. & Sally E. Johnson, married 10 Jan. 1860.

Casper, Calvin & Luvena Powell, married 28 May 1857; George
Casper, Anderson Casper, John Laseter, wit.

Casper, George & Polly Bass, 28 Jan. 1848; Cornelius Huff,
Bm.

Casper, Gordon & Maria Evans, married 20 Dec. 1866.

Casper, Thomas, Jr. & Mary Elizer Parker, married 10 Dec.
1861; W. D. Mitchell, James Burdan, A. Jenkins, wit.

Casper, Wm. & Margaret Donnison, married 14 Mar. 1867.

Casper, William, Jun. & Sally A. Hoggard, married 3 Feb.
1858; James Burden, Andrew J. Dunning, Asa F. Early, wit.

Castellaw, Harry & Caroline Miller, 21 June 1839; Asa (X)
Castellaw, Bm.

Castellaw, Henry D. & Sally Spruil, 28 Sept. 1831; James
(X) Davis, Bm.; Wm. Watford, wit.

Castellaw, James & Elizabeth Cobb, 19 July 1791; Thomas
Boswell, Bm.

BERTIE MARRIAGES, 1762-1868

Castellaw, John & Penelopey Mitchel, 30 Nov. 1785; Joseph (X) Mitchel, Bm.

Castellaw, William & Sarah Mitchel, 31 Mar. 1784; Curbey Butler, Bm.

Castellow, David & Rebecca Wilson, married 31 Jan. 1867; Marcus Butler, Isaiah Castellow, wit.

Castellow, Dossey & Penelope Hoggard, married 18 Jan. 1855.

Castellow, James & Sally Cole, 12 Aug. 1850; Noah (X) Conner, Bm.

Castellow, James & Nancy Hughs, married 21 May 1856.

Castellow, Reddin H. & Elizabeth Phelps, married 30 Oct. 1860; Thomas Grigory, David H. Lawrence, wit.

Castellow, Thos. I. & Elizabeth Castellow, married 9 Jan. 1862; Thomas H. Cobb, James Castellow, Wm. Rhodes, Shillington Ward, wit.

Castellow, Tristram & Priscilla Byram, married 9 Nov. 1855.

Castellow, Williams & Hester Lane (?), 8 Sept. 1851; Starkey Byram, Bm.

Castelow, Aquilla & Sarah Ellis, married 14 Apr. 1864; Wm. Z. Mitchell, Franklin V. Mitchell, Joseph Jenkins, Jos. Gatling (of Northampton Co.), wit.

Castelow, James (X) & Kiddy Hoggard, 16 Feb. 1827; Irrha Tayloe, C. Capehart, Bm.

Caswell, Samuel & Elizabeth Freeman, 4 Sept. 1805; Wm. (X) Perry, John Holley, Bm.

Caven, John & Sarah South, 2 Aug. 1803; Miles Bonner, Bm.

Chamberlain, Malicha (X) & Ann Harrell, 23 Mar. 1779; George Williams, Bm.

Chambers, Benjamin & Elizabeth Clifton, 13 Feb. 1775; Levin Clifton, Bm.

Champion, Joab & Sarah Rascoe, 24 Dec. 1796; William Sutton, Bm.

Champion, Zacheris & Sally Holder, 10 Sept. 1805; Charles Hardy, Bm.

Chapel, Wm. T. & Martha Moore, 17 Jan. 1853; Edward Bazemore, Bm.; Wm. Peele, Edward Bazemore, Kenneth Butler, wit. Married 18 Jan. 1853.

Chaplin, George (X) & Chloe Blount, 5 Sept. 1777; Thomas Watson, Bm.; David Standley, wit.

Chappel, Absalom (X) & Ann Cowan, 12 May 1805 (?); Ezekiel Sowell, Bm.

Chappel, Absolum (X) & Nancy Sowell, 9 Dec. 1802; Ezekiel Sowell, Bm.

Cherry, Aaron & Elizabeth Harmon, 3 Nov. 1852; Wm. J. Cherry, Bm; Jeramiah Bunch, Junr., Richard T. Harmon, Charles Harmon, wit. Married 4 Nov. 1852.

Cherry, Doctrine & Sally Ann Outlaw, 12 May 1849; Aaron Cherry, Bm.

Cherry, Dorsey & Maria Harman, married 31 Mar. 1867.

Cherry, James R. & Elizabeth Burdan, married 10 Aug. 1865.

Cherry, Joseph W. & Penaritta Pritchard, married 6 Dec. 1859.

Cherry, Noah (Col.) & Rosa A. Cherry (Col.), married 26 Dec. 1868.

Cherry, Solomon & Mary Eason, 24 Sept. 1779; David Outlaw, Bm.

Cherry, Theophilus & Kida Elizur Outlaw, married 17 Mar. 1865.

Cherry, Thomas (X) & Rachel Outlaw, 7 Jan. 1794; James Warren, Bm.

Cherry, Thomas & Jane Mitchell, 8 Oct. 1851; Jeremiah Bunch, Jr., Bm.

Cherry, Wm. & Peggy Baker, 13 Nov. 1801; Wm. Cherry, Bm.

Cherry, Wm. (Col.) & Phyllis Capehart (Col.), married 8 Mar. 1867.

Cherry, William W. & Mary Etheridge, 6 Aug. 1827; David (?) Russell, Bm.

Church, Allen & Ellen Turner, married 16 July 1855.

Church, Edward (X) & Mary Harrell, 17 Mar. 1799; Nathan (X) Page, Bm.

Church, Wm. & Mary Watson, 25 Jan. 1794; Thos. Church, Bm.

Churchwell, Allen (X) & Nancy Cuff, 23 Dec. 1802; John Mitchell, Bm.

BERTIE MARRIAGES, 1762-1868

Churchwell, Allen (X) & Winnefred ____, 7 June 1809;
Jesse Hodges, Bm.

Churchwell, Henry & Rachel Spivey, 4 Feb. 1780; William
Harrell, Bm.

Clark, Christopher & Hannah Turner, 17 Jan. 1773; Thos.
Turner, John Johnston, Bm.

Clark, David & Sarah Thompson, married 11 Aug. 1866.

Clark, George B. & Margaret E. Clark, 12 June 1858 (lic.).
Married 13 June 1858.

Clark, John & Thamar Welch, 18 Mar. 1780; Cornelius Gale,
James Johnson, Bm.

Clark, Jubiter & Peny Williams, married 3 June 1866.

Clark, Thomas & Amelia Gray, 24 Dec. 1766; Joseph Wright,
Daniel Worley, Bm.

Clary, Willie G. & Eliza B. Watson, 6 Nov. 1849; Jona S.
Tayloe, Bm.

Clayton, Wm. B. & Louisa E. Garrett, 19 Oct. 1857 (lic.).
Married 4 Nov. 1857.

Clifton, John & Penelope Ward, _____1773; Thos. Ward,
Joshua Freeman, Bm.

Clifton, William & Elizabeth W____, 29 July 1773; Thomas
Hunter, Bm.

Cobb, Elisha (X) & Sarah Lucas, 1 Apr. 1802; Samuel (X)
Misel, Bm.

Cobb, George W. & Celia A. Henry, married 30 Apr. 1867.

Cobb, George W. & Martha M. Shaw, married 5 Mar. 1868.

Cobb, Hardy & Jersey Cale, 27 Aug. 1832; Jesse Bowen, Bm.

Cobb, Harmon W. & Prudence Bowers, 20 Jan. 1825; Cornelius
Bowen, Bm.

Cobb, Henry & Sarah Kington, 1 May 1792; John Capehart, Bm.

Cobb, James & Nancy Lawrence, 10 May 1805; Thomas Cobb, Bm.

Cobb, James & Betsey Hoggard, 16 Sept. 1850; Starkey E.
Mizel, Bm.

Cobb, James H. & Edith Perry, married 19 Sept. 1855.

Cobb, James H. & Pernecia Hughs, 10 Mar. 1863 (lic.).
Married 12 Mar. 1863.

Cobb, Jno. H. & Harriet Castelow, 28 Apr. 1821; James (X)
McGlauhon, Bm.

Cobb, Nathan (X) & Winny Michel, 9 Aug. 1779; James Pritchard, Bm.

Cobb, Sam & Sarah Mizell, 4 Sept. 1852; Starkey Mizell,
Bm.; W. M. Mitchell, wit. Married 9 Sept. 1852; Starkey
E. Meezels, William Meezels, Thomas Meezels, wit.

Cobb, Thomas & Darcas Bowen, 12 Dec. 1803; Joshua (X) Bowen,
Bm.

Cobb, Thomas & Huldah Bowen, 22 May 1828; John (X) Kuhn (?),
Bm.

Coburn, Eliazer & Mary Temperance Butler, married 15 Oct.
1857.

Cochran, John & Ann Smith, 22 May 1787; John (X) Davidson,
Bm.

Coffee, Joseph & Frances Cooper, 20 Dec. 1794; Edward Manning, Bm.

Coffield, Benjamin & Nancy Carter, 11 Jan. 1808; George D.
Harrell, Bm.

Coffield, Benjamin (X) & Patsey Lasiter, 1 Mar. 1808;
Isaac Coffield, Bm.

Coffield, David James & Eliza Ann Williams, 31 Mar. 1866
(lic.). Married 1 May 1866.

Coffield, George & Elizabeth Cullipher, married 3 Mar.
1859.

Coffield, Henry & Harriet Outlaw, married 15 July 1866.

Coffield, James & Martha Ann Morris, married 7 Sept. 1865.

Coffield, Jethro & Elizabeth Butler, 25 Apr. 1788; Joseph
Simons, Bm.

Coffield, Josiah & Lydia Speight, 28 Aug. 1790; William
Coffield, Bm.

Coffield, Thomas B. & Mary Coffield, married 26 Dec. 1856.

Coffield, William & Sally Phelps, 10 July 1790; John Morgan,
Bm.

BERTIE MARRIAGES, 1762-1868

Cole, Jeremiah & Margaret Dowers, 1 June 1778; James Jones, Bm.

Cole, Jery & Elisabeth __ardy, 26 July 1807; Wm. Turner, Bm.

Cole, William & Sarah Perry, 5 July 1769; John Perry, Junr., Bm.

Collins, Andrew & Mary Barnes, 26 June 1805; John (X) Adkerson, Bm.

Collins, James & Martha Luten, married 19 Apr. 1857.

Collins, Jesse & Sarah Keen, 18 May 1802; Wm. Sowell, Bm.; Will. Cherry, wit.

Collins, Joseph & Fanny Bazemore, 7 Oct. 1787; James (X) Wilford, Bm.

Collins, Jos. & Angelica Brown, 3 Nov. 1792; Robert Hendry, Bm.

Collins, Prince A. (Col.) & Mariah James, married 28 Dec. 1868.

Collins, Thos. & Hannah Holladay, 31 Mar. 1795; John (X) Drizzle, Bm.

Combes, David & Raches Garrett, 6 July 1805; Aaron (X) Brogden, Bm.; T. Spence, Jr., wit.

Combes, Jesse & Betsey Allen, 20 Dec. 1823; Wm. (X) Overton, Bm.

Combes, Jesse & Betsey Brogden, 1 Jan. 1824; Wm. (X) Overton, Bm.

Combs, Jesse (X) & Mary Brogden, 26 Nov. 1799; John (X) Skiles, Bm.; Ams. Blount, wit.

Cone, Thomas & Celey Dunning, 10 Nov. 1801; Wm. Burlingham, Bm.

Cone, William & Mary Parker, 7 Oct. 1833; Samuel (X) Williams, Bm.

Conley, Peter M. & Jersey Wilford, 7 July 1827; Mat B. Palmer, Bm.

Conly, Peter M. & Harriet Green, 15 Mar. 1828; Will Sandrum, Bm.

Conner, Abner (X) & Eliza Dempsey, 24 Oct. 1850; Lonsor Asbell, Bm.

Conner, Andrew J. & Marina E. Conner, married 18 Feb. 1857.

Conner, Andrew J. & Rebecca Conner, married 2 Aug. 1868.

Conner, John & Mary Ellen Baker, 18 Dec. 1865 (lic.).
Married 26 Dec. 1865.

Conner, Joseph & Elizabeth Byrum, 16 May 1858 (lic.).
Married 17 May 1858.

Conner, Noah & Harriet Castellow, 9 Feb. 1833; John H.
Rhodes, Bm.

Conner, Wm. & Lavinia Minton, 14 Feb. 1831; Wright Conner,
Bm.

Conner, William & M. J. Minton, 19 Aug. 1865 (lic.).
Married 21 Aug. 1865.

Conner, William H. & Martha Ann Dunning, married 3 July
1865.

Conner, Wright & Kiddy Baker, 13 Aug. 1805; Luke (X)
Parker, Bm.

Cook, Benjamin (X) & Winnefred Hoppkins, 25 Apr. 1774;
John Hopkins, Bm.

Cook, Benjamin & Sarah E. Harrell, married 2 Jan. 1852.

Cook, Cullen & Penelope Boyce, 23 July 1795; Saml. Powell,
Bm.

Cook, Elisha (X) & Tabitha Cook, 5 May 1797; John Cook, Bm.

Cook, James & Sarah Earley, 3 Mar. 1795; John Mitchell, Bm.

Cook, Joel & Bellison Floyd, 26 Mar. 1784; Ruben (X)
Hattian, Bm.

Cook, Joel & Patience Brassell, 9 May 1797; Rubbin (X)
Cook, Bm.

Cook, Silas & Lidia Earley, 13 Feb. 1796; James Cook, Bm.

Cook, Thomas & Sarah Hopkins, 7 Jan. 1793; Thomas Harden,
Bm.

Cook, William & Ann Banon, 29 Nov. 1797; James Banon, Bm.

Cook, William (X) & Elisabeth Floyd, 24 Mar. 1801; Jonas
Rawls, Bm.

Cooke, Alfred & Martha Glessone, 3 Apr. 1828; Whitmell
Higgs, Bm.

Cooper, Blount & Jinnette Phillaw, 27 July 1799; John Lister, Bm.

Cooper, Cader, Senr. & Nancy O. Jernigan, 12 Nov. 1803; Miles Bonner, Bm.

Cooper, David & Mary Tayloe, married 3 May 1866.

Cooper, David & Caroline Casper, married 22 June 1866.

Cooper, Jesse (X) & Rachel Chapel, 24 Apr. 1795; Israel (X) Outhouse, Bm.

Cooper, John & Sally Leggett, 4 Feb. 1797; Belson Kittrell, Bm.

Cooper, John D. & Nancy Rigsby, married 12 Apr. 1860; N. Rhodes, B. Gillam, wit.

Cooper, John W. & C. P. Wheeler, married 30 Apr. 1868.

Cooper, Joseph & E. T. Sutton, 24 Dec. 1850; T. E. Fanning, Bm.

Cooper, Robert & Betsey Scott, 28 Dec. 1865 (lic.). Married 25 Jan. 1866.

Cooper, William (X) & Elisabeth Eperson, 9 Aug. 1780; Henry Smith, Bm.

Cooper, William & Mary J. Casper, married 3 Oct. 1865.

Cooper, Zena & Mariah Cooper, married 29 Jan. 1867.

Copeland, Matthias & Eliza Brewer, 21 Dec. 1853 (lic.). Married 29 Dec. 1853.

Copland, William John & Eliza Bazemore, 29 Dec. 1852; Freeman (X) Copland, Bm. Married 30 Dec. 1852.

Corbert, James (X) & Mary Hughs, 30 Oct. 1793; John Corbert, Bm.; John Harlow, wit.

Corbet, Elisha (X) & Elisabeth Cobb, 2 Nov. 1796; Hardy (X) Bowen, Bm.

Corbet, John & Tiney Wilson, 10 Aug. 1846; John White, Bm.

Corbitt, James & Susan Bryant, 19 July 1853; Henry (X) Baker, Bm. Married 19 July 1853.

Coston, Elbert & Mary E. Mebane, married 2 Nov. 1868.

Cotten, Jesse & Martha Whitehed, 6 June 1777; Wm. Rutland, Bm.

Cottle, William (X) & Elizabeth Glesson, 25 Aug. 1790;
Ephraim Rhodes, Bm.; John Wolfenden, wit.

Cowan, Jos. W. & Martha J. McGlauhon, married 14 Oct. 1867.

Cowand, Birim H. & Nancy Johnston, 29 Oct. 1827; Reuben
(X) White, Bm.

Cowand, Cullen & Judah McFarlane, 3 July 1802; Thomas (X)
Hughes, Bm.

Cowand, George & Winefred Mitchel, 21 Sept. 1791; Abraham
Duke, Bm.

Cowand, Johnson & Priscilla White, married 11 Mar. 1862.

Cowand, Jonathan & Sarah Sowell, 21 July 1800; Ezekial
Sowell, Bm.

Cowand, Joseph Worley (?) & Martha Hughs, married 3 Sept.
1856.

Cowand, Robert A. & (Mrs.) Julia Burdan, married 9 Dec.
1863.

Cowand, Solomon & Mornen Allan, 7 Oct. 1796; William (X)
Cowand, Bm.

Cowand, Wm. B. & Amanda S. Corbet, married 22 Nov. 1868.

Cox, Elisha D. & Penny Eliza Wilks, 26 Sept. 1851; Edward
Bazemore, Bm. Married _____.

Cox, Ezekial Smith & Mary Peells, 25 Sept. 1806; Moore
Higgs, Bm.

Cox, John (X) & Betsey Peal, 19 Nov. 1804; Ezekiel S. Cox,
Bm.; Kenneth Clark, wit.

Cox, John & Sarah Champion, 9 June 1805; Wm. Weston, Bm.

Cox, Reuben H. & Mary C. Askew, 13 Sept. 1853 (lic.).
Married 15 Sept. 1853.

Cox, Samuel & Sarah Francis Pritchard, married 15 Dec. 1863.

Cox, Samuel & Mary M. Rawls, married 25 Aug. 1868.

Cox, Thomas & Martha E. Garrett, 14 Nov. 1853; Wm. Bishop,
Bm. Married 17 Nov. 1853.

Coxe, Richard & Charlotte Wilkes, 10 Oct. 1837; Wilie (X)
Curry, Bm.

Craddock, Wm. & Rebecca Bowen, 10 June 1851; E. Claxton (?), Bm. Married 12 June 1851.

Craft, Herod (X) & Susanah Smith, 4 Aug. 1797; Moses (X) Caps, Bm.

Craft, Herrod & Fanny Smith, 27 Oct. 1803; Frederick Rogers, Bm.

Craig, A. M. & C. Rebecca Gillam, married 4 Dec. 1855.

Cratch, Thomas & Mazy Morgan, 15 June 1768; Jonathan Long, Wm. Armistead, Bm.; W. Nicholls, wit.

Cratch, William & Elizabeth Bate, 10 Dec. 1802; James Ray, Bm.

Cullens, Frederick & Elizabeth Wimberley, 17 Sept. 1791; Micajah Griffin, Bm.

Cullifer, Henry & Martha Glauhan, 18 Mar. 1795; John (X) Shaw, Bm.; James B. Jordan, wit.

Cullifer, Jeremiah (X) & Sarah Rogers, 30 May 1794; Thomas Seals, Bm.

Cullifer, Nathaniel (X) & Chloe Cullifer, 9 Feb. 1792; Winant Winants, Bm.

Cullifer, Nathaniel & Nancy Cullifer, 6 Aug. 1798; Jona. Jacocks, Bm.

Cullifer, Thomas (X) & Joanna Cobb, 15 Sept. 1792; John (X) Shaw, Bm.

Cullifer, William (X) & Elizabeth Barnes, 21 Jan. 1827; Wm. (X) Barnes, Bm.

Cullipher, Augustus & Asenith R. Keeter, married 15 Apr. 1866.

Cullipher, Frederick & Elizabeth Morgan, 22 Nov. 1853 (lic.). Married 23 Nov. 1854.(sic)

Cullipher, Jackson & Frances Loune (?), married 4 Sept. 1860.

Cullipher, James & Milly Ann Capps, married 3 Apr. 1856.

Cullipher, John (X) & Thamer Hawkins, 10 Jan. 1829; Nathaniel Miller, Bm.

Cullipher, Marcus (X) & Nancy Keeter, 24 Aug. 1850; Henry (X) Cullipher, Bm.

BERTIE MARRIAGES, 1762-1868

Cullipher, Marcus & Isabella Razor, married 20 Dec. 1859.

Cullipher, Marcus & Francis Cullipher, married 12 Oct. 1865.

Cullipher, Miles & Harriet Pierce, 29 Jan. 1852; William Keeter, Bm. Married 29 Jan. 1852.

Cullipher, Nathaniel & Nelly Miller, 30 May 1834; Miles Cullipher, Bm.

Cullipher, Simon & Sarah A. Piland, married 29 Oct. 1856.

Cullipher, Thomas & Lucinda Piland, married 13 Oct. 1860.

Cullipher, William E. & Sarah E. Coffield, married 18 May 1866.

Curl, Charney & Mary Hyman, 19 Apr. 1804; John Pender, Bm.

Curry, Cullen (X) & Sarah Cobb, 3 Feb. 1804; Elisha (X) Corbet, Bm.

Curry, David (X) & Sarah Wells, 23 Sept. 1780; James (X) Curry, Bm.

Curry, David, Jr. (X) & Lucy Dundston (?), 16 Sept. 1801; David (X) Curry, Bm.

Curry, James (X) & Judith Mizells, 15 Jan. 1792; Archibald (X) Wilford, Bm.; John Wolfenden, wit.

Curry, John (X) & Sarah White, 21 Dec. 1803; Willie (X) Curry, Bm.

Curry, Malachi (X) & Winefred Mesells, 20 Mar. 1805; Benajah (X) Curry, Bm.

Curry, Wilie (X) & Mornin Meezlle, 9 Dec. 1806; Bernajah (X) Curry, Bm.

Dautery, Elijah & Penelope Frame, 15 Jan. 1803; Cullen Cotten, Bm.

Davidson, David (X) & Ellenor Hinson, 25 Mar. 1788; John Bentley, Bm.

Davidson, John & Martha Smithwick, 6 Feb. 1773; John Smith, Luke Smithwick, Bm.

Davidson, John & Elizabeth Davis (widow), 23 Jan. 1777; John Legett, Edmund Dunstan, Bm.

Davis, Alpheus & Elizabeath Jenkins, married 5 Nov. 1861.

Davis, Augustus & Martha Jenkins, married 25 Apr. 1861.

BERTIE MARRIAGES, 1762-1868

Davis, David (X) & Sarah Cob, 14 Oct. 1795; Smith (X)
Davis, Bm.

Davis, Dread (X) & Nancy Belote, 2 Dec. 1794; John Cooper,
Bm.

Davis, Henry & Sarah E. Valentine, married 14 July 1868.

Davis, John & Margaret J. Thompson, married 20 June 1858.

Davis, Jonathan F. & Harriet Cullifer, married 19 Aug.
1860.

Davis, Joseph & Sarah Lawrence, 11 Apr. 1853; Thomas A.
Mardre, Bm. Married 12 Apr. 1853.

Davis, Joshua & Sarah Gardner, 12 June 1786; John Gary (?),
Bm.

Davis, Joshua (X) & Nancy Daughtery, 26 June 1832.

Davis, Lewis & Nancy Skiles, married 21 May 1856.

Davis, Merideth (X) & Ann Hooks, 29 June 1784; George
Davis, Bm.

Davis, Miles & Sarah Calloway, 26 Sept. 1798; John Williams,
Bm.

Davis, Nazareth & Phoebe Thompson, married 19 June 1858.

Davis, Smith (X) & Happy Cobb, 5 Jan. 1790; Bryan Smith, Bm.

Davis, Thomas & Elizabeth Swain, 28 Feb. 1827; William
Davis, Bm.; Jno. W. Bond, wit.

Davis, William & Sarah M. Grant, married 16 Jan. 1868.

Davison, George & Elisabeth Mcglawhan, 26 May 1803; Wright
Evans, Bm.

Dawson, James & Marcia Jordan, 11 June 1824.

Dawson, William & May Luten, 16 Oct. 1850; Solomon (X)
Page, Bm.

Dean, Samuel & Ann Church, 22 Jan. 1785; Jesse (X) Bryan,
Bm.

Deanes, Peterson & Martha Wilkes, 12 Aug. 1824; William
(X) Deanes, Bm.

Deems, Charles F. & Margaret A. Veale, 23 May 1861 (lic.).
Married 25 May 1861.

Dempsey, Abel & Celia Bunch, married 5 Dec. 1866.

Dempsey, Elisha (X) & Wealthy Dempsey, 12 Oct. 1807; Whitmell Dempsey, Bm.

Dempsey, Joseph (X) & Martha Farmer, 24 Oct. 1850.

Dempsey, Whitmell & Anna Bowen, 17 June 1806; Elisha (X)
Demsey, Bm.

Demsey, George (X) & Sally Loyd, 2 May 1797; Richard (X)
Demsey, Bm.

Demsey, Johnston (X) & Mary Jones, 5 Oct. 1833; Thomas
Burke, Bm.

Demsey, William (X) & Ann Miller, 25 July 1781; James
McDonald, Bm.

Dickson, John K. & Mary Hawkins, 18 May 1853; Littleton
Johnson, Bm. Married 19 May 1853.

Dillard, Epeneser & Annelizer Dunning, married 8 May 1864.

Dodrill, John & Elizabeth Harrel, 1 May 1778; Frederick
Hollon, James Dodrill, Bm.

Donaldson, A. Jackson & Elizabeth Barnes, married 7 Jan.
1858.

Dosier, Peter & Dorcas Nash, married 17 Mar. 1867.

Douglass, Robert & Dudith Collins, 22 June 1793; James (X)
Bazemore, Bm.

Drew, Jno. W. & Mary E. Hughs, 26 Mar. 1845; John Freeman,
Bm.

Drew, Whitmell H. & Elizabeth Butler, 13 Oct. 1827; W. H.
Green, Bm.

Drisel, John (X) & Sarah Stainback, 9 Apr. 1791; James
Rhodes, Bm.

Duers, Henry & Elizabeth Taylor, married 18 Feb. 1867.

Dundelow, John (X) & Mady Cowand, 26 Mar. 1803; George (X)
White, Bm.

Dundelow, Joseph & Nancy White, married 20 May 1866.

Duning, John & Sarah Cherry, 1 Sept. 1801; Samuel Duning,
Bm.

Duning, Uriah & Anne Earley, 17 May 1790; Job Umflet, Bm.

BERTIE MARRIAGES, 1762-1868

Duning, William & Salley Sholar, 10 Nov. 1794; Wright
Nicholls, Bm.

Dunnin, John R. (X) & Elisabeth Tayloe, 14 Jan. 1799;
James Tayloe, Bm.

Dunning, Andrew J. & Sarah Harmon, 3 Oct. 1853; Abram
Jenkens, Bm. Married 5 Oct. 1853.

Dunning, Andrew Jackson, Jr. & Winnifred Conner, 2 Feb.
1866 (lic.). Married 8 Feb. 1866.

Dunning, Charles & Elisabeth Bruce, 8 Dec. 1783; Jeremiah
Bruce, Bm.

Dunning, John & Sally Morris, 28 May 1852; David (X) Hoggard, Bm.

Dunning, Wm. C. & Mary L. Burden, married 16 Jan. 1866.

Dunston, Hannibal & Martha Williams, 26 Oct. 1866 (lic.).
Married 27 Oct. 1866.

Duval, Percy (?) R. & Agnes J. Slade, 4 Nov. 1850; Geo.
W. McGlauhan, Bm.

Earley, James (X) & Lethena Dunning, 18 Jan. 1808; Lodwick Jenkins, Bm.

Earley, John & Sallie M. Dunning, married 29 Mar. 1859.

Earley, William (X) & Esther Laton, 26 Nov. 1792; William
(X) Barradail, Bm.

Earley, William & Elisiabeth Baker, 2 Aug. 1801; Abraham
Jenkins, Bm.

Early, Abner & Eugenia Watson, married 17 Jan. 1867.

Early, Asa & Sarah Williford, 3 July 1828; James Williford,
Bm.

Early, George R. & Mason Harrell, 15 Apr. 1851; Henry L.
Mitchell, Bm. Married 15 Apr. 1851; John W. Jenkins,
Andrew J. Dunning, (Dr.) H. L. Mitchell, wit.

Early, Jasen & May Ann Harrell, married 4 Feb. 1866.

Early, Joseph S. & Mason C. Early, married 22 Jan. 1862.

Early, Sumner A. & Rena Ann Williams, married 31 July 1866.

Early, Thomas & Betsey Mitchell, 25 Sept. 1821; Lod Jinkens,
Bm.

32

BERTIE MARRIAGES, 1762-1868

Eason, George & Ann Carney, 18 Dec. 1791; Absalom Carney, Bm.; Cader Powell, wit.

Edwards, Benjamin (X) & Sarah Thomas, 5 Feb. 1787; John Edwards, Bm.

Edwards, Nathan & Jemima Cotten, 5 Sept. 1783; F. Pugh, Junr., Bm.

Edwards, William & Nancy Ward, 16 Dec. 1799; Archabald (X) Morris, Bm.

Ellenworth, Nehemiah (X) & Henneritta Bowen, 17 Dec. 1794; Abraham (X) Morris, Bm.

Ellis, Jackson & Sally Jenkins, 22 June 1857 (lic.). Married 24 June 1857.

Etheridge, William & Mary Holley, 26 Jan. 1804; Thomas Holley, Bm.

Eure, Levi & Mary Dunning, 6 Feb. 1860 (lic.). Married 9 Feb. 1860.

Evans, David D. & Milly Burden, married 29 Nov. 1866.

Evans, John & Mary Davidson, 14 Feb. 1809; Josiah (X) Harrell, Bm.

Evans, Jonas & Nancy Carter, 30 Jan. 1855 (lic.). Married 1 Feb. 1855.

Evans, Jonathan & Eliza Myers, 15 Jan. 1851; Charles H. Evans, Bm.

Evans, Marcus B. & Mary A. Rayner, married 22 Jan. 1868.

Evans, Meady (X) & Celia White, 27 Jan. 1804; Josiah (X) Harrell, Bm.

Evans, Starkey & Martha Myers, 17 Feb. 1852; Charles H. Evans, Bm. Married 19 Feb. 1852.

Evans, Wilson & Catherine Barnes, married 25 Jan. 1855.

Evarts, Luther & Sarah Hodder, 3 Aug. 1790; William Benson, Bm.

Fager, Henry C. & Mary Virginia Gillam, married 26 July 1868.

Falk, John Nazareth & Maria Roulhac, married 7 Apr. 1866.

Fanning, Thos. E. & Mary E. Pugh, 25 Sept. 1852; Harry Nicholls, Bm.

Farmer, James (X) & Anne Harmon, 17 Feb. 1784; Cader Mitchell, Bm.

Farmer, James W. & Rachel E. Outlaw, married 16 Nov. 1858; William Dunning, James Herrington, wit.

Farmer, Joseph (X) & Mary Hoggar, 6 Nov. 1799; Zadock Mitchell, Bm.

Farrow, Finch & Penelope West, 5 Oct. 1802; John (X) Moore, Bm.

Ferguson, W. A. & Mary E. Drew (?), 29 Aug. 1849; Wm. W. Bird, Bm.

Ferguson, William A. & Margaret Ann Lee, married 16 Dec. 1856.

Fife, John & Judy Thomas, 23 Mar. 1827; Wm. W. Cherry, Bm.

Fife, John (X) & Anna Harrell, 16 Apr. 1838; Geo. B. Outlaw, Bm.

Fleetwood, Edmond & Winefred Sparkman, 5 Dec. 1785; Hardy Fleetwood, Bm.

Fleetwood, George & Elizabeth Morris, 26 Apr. 1864 (lic.). Married 28 Apr. 1864.

Fleetwood, James & Penelope Taylo, 21 Oct. 1777; John Hardy, George Outlaw, Bm.

Fleetwood, Jeremiah & Sarah Fleetwood, 3 Oct. 1774; John Hardy, Bm.

Fleetwood, William & Elizabeth Ashley, 5 Oct. 1763; John (X) Ashley, Bm.

Fleetwood, William & Sarah Capehart, 19 Dec. 1792; John Fleetwood, Bm.

Flood, Grandison & Mary Baker, 26 Mar. 1858 (lic.). Married 28 Mar. 1858.

Flood, John & Celia Weaver, married 28 Feb. 1867.

Floyd, John G. & Sarah E. King, married 28 Feb. 1866.

Floyd, Randolph (X) & Judah Wair (?), 3 Aug. 1798; Thomas Sholar, Bm.

Floyd, Samuel & ____ Groves, married 27 Feb. 1868.

Folk, Benjamin & Jemima Kittrell, 4 Nov. 1797; Belson Kittrell, Bm.

BERTIE MARRIAGES, 1762-1868

Fort, John & Martha Turner, 30 Dec. 1774; John Turner,
John Robinson, Bm.

Frances, Moses D. & Elizabeth Castellow, married 27 Nov.
1858.

Francis, Benjamin & Sary Hast, married 22 Sept. 1858.

Francis, Charles H. & Martha J. Miller, married 9 Sept.
1867.

Francis, James & Delila Coffield, married 24 Jan. 1861.

Franlon, John (X) & Penelope Hayse, 23 May 1786; Jacob
(X) Bird, Bm.

Frazer, William & Drissallah Outlaw, 10 Jan. 1774; Nathan
Miers, Juner., Bm.

Freeman, Charles & Martha E. Miller, married 14 Feb. 1867.

Freeman, Daniel & Rebecca Pruden, married 2 Feb. 1867.

Freeman, George & Mary Drew, married 4 Jan. 1859.

Freeman, Hardy & Senith Hunter, 4 Apr. 1796; William Hunter, Bm.

Freeman, Henry & Rachel Freeman, married 28 Jan. 1867.

Freeman, Howell & Martha Thomas, 7 Apr. 1851; Jacob (X)
White, Bm. Married 7 Apr. 1851.

Freeman, James C. & Margaret E. Redditt, married 15 Jan.
1857.

Freeman, James H. & Martha Ann Hobbs, 3 Mar. 1863 (lic.).
Married 4 Mar. 1863.

Freeman, James P. & Mary E. White, married 28 Nov. 1867.

Freeman, Jeremiah & Mary Norflet, 9 Oct. 1792; William
Watford, Bm.

Freeman, John & Nancy Henry, 10 Aug. 1798; Aaron Freeman,
Bm.

Freeman, John & Sally Outlaw (dau. of Lewis Outlaw), 28
Dec. 1808; Reuben Harison, Bm.

Freeman, John & Harriet Adkins, married 2 Sept. 1860.

Freeman, Joseph & Elenor Lane, married 3 Aug. 1859.

Freeman, Josiah & Sarah Moore, 23 Dec. 1796; James B. Jordan,
Bm.

BERTIE MARRIAGES, 1762-1868

Freeman, Richard P. & Sarah S. J. Worley, 4 Sept. 1833;
William F. Moring, Bm.

Freeman, Riddick N. & Amanda White, married 15 Mar. 1859.

Freeman, Thomas & Hetty Cowand, married 10 Apr. 1856.

Freeman, Washington (Col.) & Winny Freeman (Col.), 7 Mar.
1868 (lic.). Married 17 Mar. 1868.

Fryer, Henderson & Delylah Williams, 6 May 1797; Isom
Wilford, Bm.

Fryer, Joseph W. & Permelia F. Blount, married 21 July
1857.

Furguson, John R. & Martha E. Gill, 21 Nov. 1850; Wm. W.
Bird, Bm.

Ganes, John & Elisabeth Loyd, 4 Sept. 1779; John Legett,
Bm.

Gardner, Bryan (X) & Anne Horton, 9 July 1795; James A.
Gardner, Bm.

Gardner, James A. & Elisabeth Turner, 12 Feb. 1799; Thomas
Bond, Bm.

Gardner, Jason & Sarah Harrell, 15 Feb. 1796; Hy. G. W.
Bates, Bm.

Gardner, John & Elisabeth James, 9 Feb. 1780; Wm. Bryan,
Bm.

Gardner, John & Mourning Lassiter, 27 Dec. 1786; Martin
(X) Gardner, Bm.; Wm. Bryan, wit.

Gardner, Thomas & Sarah Cullens, 29 Feb. 1780; Augustin
Parrott, Bm.

Gardner, William (X) & Penelope Eason, 25 Dec. 1797; Joel
Cook, Bm.

Gardner, Wm. H. & Mary E. Simmons, married 29 Nov. 1866.

Garett, Amariah & Elizabeth Copeland, 4 Oct. 1827; Samuel
G. Hyman, Bm.

Garrett, Alfred F. (of Washington Co.) & Mary C. Cotton,
married 13 Sept. 1854 by Benjn. S. Bronson, Episcopal
Minister, St. Thomas Church, Windsor.

Garrett, Everard & Elizabeth Freeman, 7 Nov. 1808; John
Leary, Bm.

Garrett, Hilliard & Betty Mizells, 20 Jan. 1866 (lic.).
Married 4 Jan. 1866.(sic)

Garrett, Jacob & Rachel Eason, 25 Dec. 1790; Jesse Garrett,
Bm.; Wm. Skiles, wit.

Garrett, Jesse & Basha Perry, 21 May 1799; Jacob Garrett,
Bm.

Garrett, Joseph & Rachel Spight, 24 Apr. 1792; John West,
Bm.

Garrett, Joshua L. & Sarah Hays, 1 Sept. 1865 (lic.).
Married 5 Sept. 1865.

Garrett, Richard & Mary A. C. Thompson, 24 Nov. 1849;
Benj. B. Williams, Bm.

Garrett, Robert F. & Jane E. Early, 14 July 1857 (lic.).
Married 19 July 1857.

Garrett, Samuel & Chloe Manning, 28 May 1785; John Bentley,
Bm.

Garrett, Thomas & Patsy Holly, 19 Aug. 1796; Jonathan
Spivey, Bm.

Garriss, W. D. (son of W. D. Garriss) & Fannie G. Hodges
(dau. of William & Mary Hodges), married 19 Nov. 1868.

Gaskins, David & Elisabeth Cofield, 21 Oct. 1790; James
Capehart, Bm.

Gaskins, David, Jr. & Ellen Cook, 23 Oct. 1833; William
Moring, Bm.; Jona. R. Webb, wit.

Gaskins, George & Peggy Madrey, 30 Mar. 1804; Charles
Hardy, Bm.

Gaskins, John & Chloe Cobb, 24 Nov. 1804; George Gaskins,
Bm.

Gaskins, Thomas & Olive Ray, 7 Dec. 1782; Alexander Hooks,
Bm.

Gaskins, Thomas (X) & Frances Rea, 13 Dec. 1826.

Gill, Henry & Christian Phelps, married 22 Apr. 1868.

Gill, William E. & Penelope C. Phelps, married 11 Oct. 1867.

Gillam, Benjamin & Sally Hardy, married 6 Aug. 1857.

Gillam, Irwin & Mema Rascoe, 14 Sept. 1866 (lic.). Married
16 Sept. 1866.

Gillam, Moses & Celea Davis, 23 June 1786; William Rhodes, Bm.

Gillam, Moses & Winefred Rhodes, 5 Nov. 1793.

Gillam, Thos. & Francis Jordan, married 14 June 1855.

Gillam, Thomas & Frances Watson, married 1 Apr. 1858.

Gilliam, (Rev.) Edward Winslow & Emily Turner Ryan, married 22 July 1863 by Cyrus Water, Rector of St. Thomas Church.

Glesson, Arthur (X) & Elisabeth Spence, 13 Apr. 1780; Micajah Hinton, Bm.

Godwin, Samuel & Christian Askew, 18 Aug. 1801; Noah Nichols, Bm.

Graham, Albert & Fanny Simons, married 12 May 1866.

Granberry,Samuel & Patsey Bailey, 18 Feb. 1820; James Rutland, Bm.

Granbery, David & Mary Moore, 11 Aug. 1802; William Johnston, Bm.

Granbery, James & Penelope Moore, 18 May 1790; Josiah Moore, Wm. Granbery, Bm.

Granbery, Langley & Salley Moore, 11 Feb. 1795; William Higgs, Bm.

Gray, Thomas & Nancy Brown, married 28 Oct. 1856.

Gray, William S. & Mary Webb, married 25 Oct. 1859.

Green, George N. & Cinthea Muzell, 24 Oct. 1850; John F. Williams, Bm.

Green, Isaac & Cynthia Outlaw, 5 Nov. 1808; John Wynns, Levy Benthall, Bm.

Green, John & Louisa Matthews, married 13 Sept. 1855.

Green, Jno. A. & Julia Evans, 19 Sept. 1849; G. N. Green, Bm.

Green, Thomas & Mary Hunt, 3 Oct. 1764; John Crickett, Bm.

Green, Thos. H. & Mary Casper, married 15 Sept. 1859.

Green, William H. & Ann Lassiter, 4 Jan. 1794; Wilson Liscombe, Bm.

Green, William H. & Peggy Outlaw, 6 Jan. 1797; William Watson, Bm.

Gregory, Alfred & Sally Ann Elliot, 8 Jan. 1862 (lic.). Married 9 Jan. 1862.

Gregory, David S. & Marthena E. Hoggard, 20 Aug. 1864 (lic.). Married 23 Aug. 1864.

Gregory, Hubbard (Col.) & Penelope Webb (Col.), married 27 Dec. 1868.

Gregory, James & Rachel Boswell, 26 Aug. 1806; Jos. H. Bryan, Bm.

Gregory, William L. & Mary Jane Perry, married 5 May 1859.

Griffin, Edward & Elizabeth Lawrence, 10 Oct. 1764; Edwd. Rasor, John Yeats, Bm.; John Lawrence, William Griffin, wit.

Griffin, King B. & Frances Mizell, 3 Jan. 1866 (lic.). Married 4 Jan. 1866.

Griffin, Thomas (X) & Esther Basemore, ____17__; Elisha (X) Sumner, Bm.

Griffin, Willie H. & Martha Thomas, 1 Mar. 1828; W. E. Bird, Bm.

Grimes, James & Catherine Veale, 29 July 1803; Richd. Veale, Bm.

Grover, Jas. S. & Elisabeth Rutland, 13 May 1799; Norsworthy Rutland, Bm.

Grover, Jas. Swinhow & Susanah Spencer, 22 Oct. 1768; William Twain, Bm.

Gurley, Wm. P. & Sarah E. Smallwood, 12 Feb. 1846; Jona. S. Tayloe, John L. Webb, Bm.

Gurley, William P. & Agnes B. Simmons, married 5 Jan. 1865.

Gurley, William P. & Ann E. McGlauhon, married 27 Mar. 1867.

Gurley, William P. & Elizabeth J. Hines, married 1 Nov. 1868.

Guyther, Jno. & Hannah Jordan, 3 July 1804; Luke Smithwick, Bm.

Hadom, Godwin Jernigan & Mary Mires, 15 Nov. 1785; George Jernigan Hadom, Wm. Wood, Bm.

BERTIE MARRIAGES, 1762-1868

Hadom, Lewis Jernagan (X) & Winefred Mires, 17 July 1792;
Samuel Jernagan (X) Hadom, Bm.

Hadom, Samuel Jernagan (X) & Rachel Farmer, 15 Nov. 1792;
Godwin Jernikin, Bm.

Hail, James (X) & Nancy Mitchell, 14 Jan. 1807; James
Mitchell, Bm.

Haile, Joseph H. & Alfreda Slade, married 7 Feb. 1864;
Willie Downs, Mary Downs, (Mrs.) A. J. Dunning, wit.

Hale, Edward & Nancy Jones, married 12 July 1859.

Hale, John & Christian Flood, married 14 Aug. 1855.

Hale, Joseph H. & Emaline Downs, 15 Oct. 1851; John W.
Jenkins, Bm. Married 16 Oct. 1851; John W. Jenkins,
Jesse Downs, Abram Jenkins, wit.

Hale, Joshua, Jr. (X) & Winefred White, 30 June 1790;
Joshua (X) Hale, Bm.

Hall, James & Elisabeth Tyner, 23 Sept. 1780; Solomon (X)
Baker, Bm.

Hall, James & Elizabeth Smith, married 29 Mar. 1857.

Hall, William & Martha C. Cook, married 30 Apr. 1866.

Halloway, Cader (X) & Judith Harrell, 2 May 1779; Whitson
Young, Bm.

Halloway, Ruben (X) & Martha Vinson, 22 May 1777; William
Toary (?), Bm.

Hallum, John (X) & Keddy Capehart, 4 Mar. 1795; Elisha
(X) Todd, Bm.

Hallum, Josiah (X) & Ann Roberson, 28 Oct. 1782; Luis
Todd, Bm.

Halsay, Cullen & Nancy Perry, married 8 Feb. 1859.

Hamlin, (Col.) Robert P. (of Northampton Co.) & (Mrs.)
Willie J. Hill, married 23 Nov. 1857 by Benjn. S. Bronson, Rector of St. Thomas Church, Windsor.

Hancock, Robert H. & Ophelia L. Peele, married 25 Jan.
1866.

Hardee, Thomas & Delila Davis, 22 Feb. 1763; Charles
Hardee, Humphry Nicholls, Bm.; L. Lockhart, wit.

Harden, Hardy L. B. & Agnes Cullipher, 1 Feb. 1852; Calvin Hogwood, Bm. Married 1 Feb. 1852.

Harden, Levi & Mary Barnacastle, 22 Mar. 1842; Geo. Washington (X) Pierce, Bm.

Harden, Martin & Winny Dunes (?), married 26 Jan. 1867.

Harden, Thomas & Sarah Sarrinn (?), 16 Apr. 1777; John Smith, Bm.

Harden, Thomas & Nancy Capehart, 16 May 1800; Josiah Redditt, Bm.

Harden, Thomas & Priscilla Pearce, 15 Aug. 1801; Mathew (X) Pearce, Bm.

Harden, William D. & Henrietta F. Tinch, married 1 Apr. 1866.

Hardy, Edward & Winefred Weston, 6 Jan. 1765; William Hardy, Lemuel Hardy, Jno. F. Lamber, Bm.; Sarah (X) Hardy, wit.

Hardy, Humy. & Mourning Smith (widow), 19 Mar. 1764; Hump. Nicholls, Alexr. How, Bm.; Elizth. How, wit.

Hardy, Jackson & Sophia Askew, 14 May 1866.

Hardy, James & Betsey Gaskins, 30 Sept. 1788; John (X) Bird, Bm.

Hardy, James W. & May R. Simmons, 15 Jan. 1866 (lic.). Married 17 Jan. 1866.

Hardy, John & Jamima Wilson, 9 Apr. 1793; Stephen Buck, Bm.; Frances Gray, wit.

Hardy, John & Elizabeth Ward, 15 Nov. 1798; Stephen Buck, Bm.; Kenneth Clark, wit.

Hardy, John & Dililah Spivy, married 14 Mar. 1867.

Hardy, Joseph & Nancy Hoggard, 19 Sept. 1787; Silas Belote, Bm.

Hardy, Joseph H. & Louisa Camilla Bishop, married 2 Oct. 1860 by Jos. Blount Cheshire, Rector of Trinity Church, Scotland Neck, N. C.

Hardy, Lamb & Winefred Boswell, 23 Aug. 1790; Charles Boswell, Bm.

Hardy, Madison & Anarchy Norfleet, married _____1866 (?).

41

Harison, King & Jenney White, 29 Mar. 1786; King White, Bm.

Harison, Reuben & Ann Mitchell, 18 May 1790; George Harison, Bm.

Harman, James F. & Martha Jane Todd, married 23 Jan. 1866.

Harman, Michel & Elizabeth Moore, 2 Dec. 1803; Nicholas (X) Harman, Bm.

Harman, Nicholas (X) & Anne Dunning, 3 Nov. 1802; Benjamin Yearley, Bm.

Harman, Riddick H. & Bittie Burdan, married 8 Feb. 1866.

Harmon, Enoch & Martha Harmon, 8 July 1852; Wm. J. Cherry, Bm. Married 8 July 1852; Nehemiah J. Bunch, Charles W. Harmon, Eli Harmon, wit.

Harmon, Stephen & Judy Farmer, 26 Oct. 1790; James (X) Farmer, Bm.

Harrell, Alanson & Margaret Minton, married 16 Aug. 1865.

Harrell, Alexander & Mary Burress, married 16 Feb. 1865.

Harrell, Amos & Charity Rutland, 8 Nov. 1774; Benjamin Harrell, Bm.

Harrell, Amos (X) & Zilpha Harrell, 18 May 1808; Thomas Harrell, Bm.

Harrell, Benjamin & Winnefred Pitman (?), 2 June 1774; Amos Harrell, Bm.

Harrell, Benjamin H. (X) & Mary Ann Britt, 20 Oct. 1849; John Parker, Bm.

Harrell, David & Celia Moor, 10 May 1777; Noah Thompson, Bm.

Harrell, (Rev.) David & Elizabeth Dale, married 26 Oct. 1854.

Harrell, David & Ann M. Hobbs, married 27 Dec. 1866.

Harrell, Don Carlos & Mary Thomas, married 27 Feb. 1855; Richard R. Tayloe, Jesse Bazemore, Kenneth Butler, wit.

Harrell, Gabriel & Frances Harrell, 22 Dec. 1798; Jason Gardner, Bm.

Harrell, George & Martha Blanchard, 28 May 1804; William White, Bm.; Kenneth Clark, wit.

Harrell, George E. & Maria Frances Mizell, married 2 Jan. 1868.

Harrell, George J. & Mary E. Bond, 24 June 1854 (lic.). Married 28 June 1854.

Harrell, Guing (X) & Elizabeth Kittrell, 23 Aug. 1790; Solomon (X) Page, Bm.

Harrell, H. P. & Elizabeth Tyler, 20 Jan. 1862 (lic.). Married 21 Jan. 1862.

Harrell, Henry (X) & Annis Davis, 10 Mar. 1788; John Wimberley, Bm.

Harrell, Hughes (X) & Mary McDowell, 17 Dec. 1792; Nathan (X) Smith, Bm.

Harrell, Isaac & Mary Catharine Bird, married 18 Mar. 1858.

Harrell, Isaac Norfleet & Margaret Ann Francis, 9 Nov. 1866 (lic.). Married 10 Nov. 1866.

Harrell, Isom (X) & Judah Peele, 1 Jan. 1800; Joel (X) Jones, Bm.

Harrell, James (X) & Elizabeth Lane, 15 Feb. 1809; Elijah Rayner, Bm.

Harrell, James H. & Mary E. Peele, 3 Jan. 1859 (lic.). Married 5 Jan. 1859.

Harrell, Jeremiah & Penelope Purvis, 22 Dec. 1800; Joel Jones, Bm.

Harrell, Jesse & Rachel Kittrell, 11 Nov. 1794; Lewis Bryan, Bm.

Harrell, Jesse & Sarah Conner, 12 Feb. 1853; Benten (X) H. Raby, Bm. Married 13 Feb. 1853.

Harrell, Jesse & Elizabeth White, married 26 Dec. 1860.

Harrell, Jesse & Elizabeth Mizell, married 3 Oct. 1867.

Harrell, Joel & Caela Goff, 20 Apr. 1779; Edward Acree, Bm.; James Blake, wit.

Harrell, Joel & Elizabeth Shoular, 7 June 1801; Solomon Sholar, Bm.

Harrell, John & Mary Barfield, 22 Dec. 1785; Joseph Horne, Bm.

Harrell, John & Lavina Hobbs (dau. of Silas Hobbs), married 5 Dec. 1867.

Harrell, John B. & Sarah Jane Livermore, married 26 Dec. 1865.

Harrell, John L. & Mary Williams, married 11 Feb. 1866.

Harrell, John W. & Repsey Hobdy (?), 27 Jan. 1792; John Rutland, Bm.

Harrell, Jonathan & Elizabeth Gardner, 18 Aug. 1787; William Rascoe, Bm.

Harrell, Joseph (X) & Polly Gaskins, 6 May 1809; Elijah Rayner, Bm.

Harrell, Josiah & Mary Ann Gardner, 13 Dec. 1777; William Rasco, Bm.

Harrell, Josiah & Sarah Harrell, 21 Sept. 1778; Josiah Harrell, Sr., Bm.

Harrell, Josiah (X) & Mary Irvings (?), 21 Jan. 1783; Luke (X) White, Bm.

Harrell, Josiah (X) & Sarah Evans, 26 Mar. 1805; John Dawson, Bm.

Harrell, Josiah (X) & Mary Evans, 14 Feb. 1809; John Evans, Bm.

Harrell, Lewis & Sarah Canady, 17 Dec. 1798; James Harrell, Bm.

Harrell, Luke (X) & _____Brannet, 14 Aug. 1805; James Brannet, Bm.

Harrell, Matthew & Susanda Conner, married 7 Jan. 1857.

Harrell, Michael D. & Martha R. Perry, married 23 Dec. 1868.

Harrell, Noah (X) & Patience Cross, 11 Feb. 1789; Joel Harrell, Bm.

Harrell, Powell & Harriet Rice, 3 May 1834; David (X) Harrell, Bm.

Harrell, Riddick & Martha J. Askew, married 5 Mar. 1856.

Harrell, Starkey J. & Mary Ann Askew, 9 Nov. 1830; George Askew, Bm.

Harrell, Thomas & Ann Burket, 26 Sept. 1792; William Rhodes, Bm.

Harrell, Thos. J. & Sally F. Butler, married 20 Jan. 1867.

Harrell, William & Edey White, 20 Jan. 1787 (lic.).

Harrell, William J. & Rebecca Ann Williams, married 16 Dec. 1866; Wm. H. Butler, Thomas J. Harrell, wit.

Harrill, Benjamin & Jemima Powell, 23 Mar. 1775; George Powell, Bm.

Harris, John & Leeda Cullipher, married 8 Apr. 1855.

Harris, Thomas & Nancy Davis, married 2 June 1859.

Harris, Thos. & Mary Ann Hoggard, married 31 Jan. 1861.

Harrison, K. D. & Hester Williford, married 5 June 1866.

Harrison, Reuben (X) & Mary Powell, 26 July 1853 (lic.). Married 30 Sept. 1853.

Harrison, Reuben & Susan Williams, married 15 Aug. 1867.

Harrison, Thomas & Frances Lister, 20 Apr. 1780; Samuel Milburn, Bm.

Harriss, Thomas & Elisabeth Bosman, 14 Apr. 1801; Saml. R. Clarkson, Bm.

Haskins, Frank & Elizabeth Casper, married 3 Dec. 1867.

Hassell, A. H. & Mary A. Holder, 10 Nov. 1853; Abram Holder, Bm. Married 10 Nov. 1853; Nazareth Rhodes, Abram Holder, wit.

Hawkins, John (X) & Sarah Williams, 12 June 1797; Wm. (X) Williams, Bm.

Hawkins, William H. & Belenda Johnson, married 25 June 1862.

Hayes, Henry (X) & Suesanah Wood, 14 Nov. 1786; William (X) Wood, Bm.

Hayes, Joshua & Anne Hayes, 9 May 1792; Josiah Moor, Bm.

Hays, Samuel (X) & Mary Martin, 16 Oct. 1778; Hardy Hays, Bm.

Hays, Willie D. & Bartra Wilson, 18 Apr. 1857 (lic.). Married 19 Apr. 1857.

Haywood, John & Rebecca Palmer, 26 Dec. 1826; Geo. B. Outlaw, Bm.

Haze, Lodwick & Mary Jenkins, 6 Jan. 1827; Lodwick (X) Jenkins, Bm.

45

BERTIE MARRIAGES, 1762-1868

Heckstall, John W. & Ann E. Tadlock, married 20 Sept. 1854; Thos. Beasly, James Heckstall, Theodore Heckstall, wit.

Hedgepeth, Marmaduke & Hannah Hays, 29 Sept. 1777; James Hayes, Bm.

Hendricks, Wm. S. & Eleanor M. Parker, married 10 Dec. 1868.

Hendry, William & Martha Oxley, 24 Jan. 1792; John Oxley, Bm.

Heninbury (?), Peter & Francis A. Simmons, 28 Dec. 1852; G. W. McGlauhan, Bm.

Henry, Hampton & Harriet Hobbs, 11 Jan. 1834; E. Reed, Bm.

Henry, James & Sarah Sowell, 22 Jan. 1808; Demsey Boyce, Bm.

Henry, John & Maria White, 17 Sept. 1850; Augustus Gaskins, Bm.

Henry, Richard R. & Adaline J. Gaskins, married 20 Jan. 1857.

Hermon, Abraham & Teresa Tayloe, 12 Sept. 1796; James Tayloe, Bm.

Herrington, James & Sarah M. Outlaw, married 2 July 1868.

Hicks, John & Sarah Roberson, 16 Sept. 1786; John Leming, Bm.

Higgins, Joseph & Dorcas Flood, 5 Oct. 1853.

Higgs, John & Milley Moore, 16 May 1786; Benjn. Mires, Bm.

Higgs, John (X) & Betty Higgs, 29 Dec. 1787; Henry (X) Vann, Bm.

Higgs, Reuben & Judah Hayse, 25 July 1800; William Peel, Bm.

Higs, William & Deliley More, 17 Jan. 1782; Willis Powell, Bm.

Hill, _____ & Mary E. Outlaw, 9 Jan. 1850; John Hill, Bm.

Hill, Hardy & Jeaney Bryant, 20 Jan. 1775; Thomas Collins, Andrew Oliver, Bm.; P. Stewart, wit.

Hill, John (X) & Senith Robertson, 4 Jan. 1804; Reuben (X) Miller, Bm.

Hill, John & William J. Ruffin, 21 Oct. 1851; Wm. Hill, Bm. Married 23 Oct. 1851 by Jos. Blount Cheshire, Rector of Calvary Church, Tarboro, N. C.

Hill, Stephen, Jr. & Wm. Edward Hardy, married 27 Jan. 1866.

Hill, Thomas & Mary Boon, 12 July 1780; George Wair, Bm.

Hindsley, John & Ann Stone, 7 Mar. 1807; Will Copeland, Bm.

Hines, Benjamin & Anna Pritchard, married 17 Dec. 1866.

Hines, Richard (of Edenton) & Margaret Norfleet, married 19 Jan. 1858 by Benj. S. Bronson, Rector of St. Thomas Church, Windsor.

Hinton, I. R. & Caroline Morris, married 12 Aug. 1864.

Hinton, John W. & Adaline White, 31 Jan. 1852; Turner Wilson, Bm. Married 3 Feb. 1852.

Hinton, Reuben & Rachel Baker, 10 Nov. 1792; Wright Williford, Bm.

Hinton, William & Anne Turner, 7 Mar. 1770; Jonathan Car, Bm.

Hoard, Wiley & Mary E. Stallings, married 23 Sept. 1861.

Hobbs, Moses & Martha Smith, 25 Jan. 1854; Thomas (X) Smith, Bm.

Hobbs, Samuel (X) & Tempy Collins, 9 Oct. 1805; John (X) Byrd, Bm.

Hobs, Quinten & Margaret Pugh, married 4 July 1855.

Hodder, James & Sally Lednum, 13 June 1827; Samuel South, Bm.

Hodder, James O. & Elenor Bayly, married 20 Oct. 1867.

Hogard, Wright (X) & Amelia Tyner, 23 May 1793; William Hogard, Bm.

Hoggard, Asa & Susan Evans, 20 Jan. 1851; Joseph (X) Hobbs, Bm.

Hoggard, Blount & Lucy Tayloe, 15 Mar. 1866 (lic.). Married 19 Mar. 1866; W. P. Mitchell, wit.

Hoggard, Calvin & Rebecca Miller, 21 Feb. 1854; Frasieur Hoggard, Bm. Married 22 Feb. 1854.

Hoggard, Calvin & Margaret A. Smithwick, 22 Dec. 1858 (lic.). Married 23 Sept. 1858.(sic)

Hoggard, David & Sally Meizells, 3 Jan. 1824; John Mizell, Bm.; James Allen, wit.

Hoggard, David & Mary Jernigan, 11 Oct. 1853; John Hoggard, Bm. Married 13 Oct. 1853.

Hoggard, David & Mary Brown (dau. of Rowan Brown), married 11 Sept. 1867.

Hoggard, Drew & Patsey Miers, 17 July 1827; Lewis Spivey, Bm.

Hoggard, Edwd. & Penny Cullipher, 29 Nov. 1828; Cullen (X) Bunch, Bm.

Hoggard, Edwd. & Mary Marshall, 2 Oct. 1834; Aaron S. Mezells, Bm.

Hoggard, Elisha (X) & Milley White, 21 May 1798; Reuben (X) Harrison, Bm.

Hoggard, Elisha & Winney Cobb, 3 Sept. 1804; Jacobb White, Bm.

Hoggard, Elisha & Emiline Mizell, married 31 May 1860; Moses S. Mizell, David H. Lawrence, wit.

Hoggard, Emsley & Eliza Britt, 14 Mar. 1839; William Watson (?), Bm.

Hoggard, Emsly & Mary Williams, 10 Sept. 1853; Jethro (X) Matthias, Bm. Married 11 Sept. 1853; Fredrick White, Joseph Williams, wit.

Hoggard, Frazier & Elizabeth White, 13 Jan. 1858 (lic.). Married 17 Jan. 1858.

Hoggard, George & Elizabeth Williams, married 12 Nov. 1854; Wm. Hoggard, W. C. Miller, wit.

Hoggard, James & Jane Rice, married 1 Oct. 1857; Jacob Pruden, Dorsey Rice, John Rice, wit.

Hoggard, Jesse (X) & Elizabeth Mires, 29 Dec. 1792; Patrick (X) Hoggard, Bm.

Hoggard, Jesse & Nelly Brogdon, 27 Jan. 1831; Seth (X) Hoggard, Bm.

Hoggard, Jesse J. & Abba Pritchard, married 16 Nov. 1854; Jer. H. Bunch, Joseph J. Bridger, Joseph W. Drew, wit.

Hoggard, John & Pennyritta Jernigan, married 14 Feb. 1856.

Hoggard, John & (Mrs.) Mary Ann Hassell, married 22 Nov. 1866.

Hoggard, Joseph & Penny Mizell, 20 Nov. 1851; Charles H. Evans, Bm.

Hoggard, Thomas & Nancy Bazemore, married 14 May 1857.

Hoggard, Timothy & Cary Castallow, married 24 Mar. 1858.

Hoggard, William & Pernicia Morriss, 24 Nov. 1851; Joseph B. Spivey, Bm.

Hoggard, William & Rachel Pritchard, married 11 Oct. 1854; Jeremiah H. Bunch, Calvin Casper, wit.

Hoggard, Wm. J. & Thena Parker, married 1 Nov. 1865.

Hoggard, Wm. P. & Nancy C. Wynns, married 8 ___1868 (?).

Hoke, John & Nancy Ford, married 24 Feb. 1866.

Holder, Aaron (X) & Drucilla Moore, 10 Apr. 1798; James (X) Williams, Bm.

Holder, Abram & Amanda E. Bunch, married 24 Jan. 1866.

Holder, Docton P. & Sarah E. Thompson, married 19 June 1860.

Holder, Elisha & Winefred Bunch, 4 June 1792; John Corbert, Bm.

Holder, Ezekiel & Mary Pruden, 10 Nov. 1807; D. Pruden, Bm.

Holder, James H. & Elizabeth Hoggard, married 16 Jan. 1866.

Holder, Shadrack (X) & Minney Duning, 4 Feb. 1799; Micajah (X) Bunch, Bm.

Holder, Thomas (X) & Anne Tayloe, 28 July 1795; David Pruden, Bm.

Holder, Wm. A. & Francis Rhodes, married 23 Nov. 1858.

Holiday, William A. (of Martin Co.) & Martha C. Mizells, married 23 Nov. 1854; Samuel Floyd, Robert Bridger, Thomas Casper, wit.

Holladay, John & Tempy Boswell, 13 July 1809; John Legett, Bm.

Holland, Frederick & Grace Cole, 9 Jan. 1792; Joshua Sholar, Bm.; Wm. Bryan, wit.

Holland, John & Sarah Higgs, 10 Feb. 1784; Willis Callum, Bm.

Holland, Walter B. & Mary E. Cooper, married 27 May 1868.

Holland, William & Ann Bowen, 19 May 1768; James Knott, Bm.

BERTIE MARRIAGES, 1762-1868

Holley, John & Patsey Outlaw, 7 Jan. 1806; James Briton, Bm.

Holley, More & Catherine Wilson, 16 Nov. 1797; Jacob Outlaw, Bm.

Holley, Thomas & Sealah Askew, 20 Dec. 1802; Josiah Holley, Bm.

Holloman, Jestine & Sarah Hagathay, 27 Feb. 1858 (lic.). Married 4 Mar. 1858.

Holloman, Wm. H. & Harriet Perry, 25 Aug. 1857 (lic.). Married 28 Aug. 1857.

Hollomon, Samuel (X) & Betsy Earley, 11 Mar. 1798; Abner Williford, Bm.

Hollowell, Arthur & Elisabeth Sharrock, 12 Jan. 1797; William Hollowell, Bm.

Hopkins, Alexander & Morin Brown, 10 Feb. 1796; Izreal (?) Yeates, Bm.

Hopkins, Collin & Nancy Rayner, 30 May 1833; Jona. S. Tayloe, Wm. Watford, Bm.

Hopkins, Daniel & Frances Cobb, 20 Nov. 1793; Noah Belote, Bm.

Hopkins, John & Jennet Stewart, 23 Apr. 1774; Benjamin (X) Cook, Bm.

Horne, Joseph & Barbara Harrell, 18 Apr. 1778; Moses Horne, Bm.

Hornsby, Samuel & Winnafred Moore, 1 Apr. 1827; John Stewart, Bm.

Horten, Henry & Elisabeth Boulton, 24 July 1784; Wm. Parrot Hardy, Bm.

Horton, Jordon I. & Permelia Bishop, married 19 Mar. 1867.

Houlder, James & Elizabeth Gelmon, 15 May 1766; Robt. Butterton, Bm.

House, Baliss & Penelope Bond, 5 Apr. 1784; Thomas Bond, Bm.

House, George & Lydia Gray, 5 July 1793; Nathan (X) Page, Bm.

Howard, Benjamin & Elisabeth Jinkins, 2 Jan. 1784; Lewis Jinkins, Bm.

Howard, Elijah & Urodilla Rhodes, 10 May 1803; Benjamin (X) Howard, Bm.

Howard, Elisha (X) & Loue Baker, 8 Sept. 1787; Richard
Baker, Bm.

Howard, Grandison & Elizabeth Grant, married 27 Dec. 1866.

Howell, James & Susannah Twain, 10 Sept. 1788; Latchworth
Twain, Bm.

Howell, Joseph & Rebecca Rhodes, 21 Feb. 1803; Leincestan
Vaughan, Bm.

Howell, Josiah & Sarah Lassiter, 2 Jan. 1787; Thomas Carney, Bm.

Hubbell, Walter & Mary Ventures, 22 May 1790; John Wolfenden, Bm.

Hughes, Charles & Sally Mott, 20 Jan. 1784; Zedh. Stone, Bm.

Hughes, Cornelius & Mary Murray, 24 Feb. 1804; James Todd,
Bm.

Hughes, Henry (X) & Mary Allen, 22 Jan. 1839; Meedy White,
Bm.

Hughes, John & Martha Myers, married 27 June 1866.

Hughes, John H. & Martha A. Perry, married 4 June 1868.

Hughs, Augustus & Kiddy M. Perry, married 22 Jan. 1861.

Hughs, Cornelius & Sophia Jane Lassiter, 26 May 1862 (lic.).
Married 29 May 1862.

Hughs, George (X) & Henneretta Morris, 15 Jan. 1787; James
Hughs, Bm.

Hughs, George R. & Elizabeth Perry, married 2 Mar. 1856.

Hughs, Henry & Charlot White, 15 Nov. 1806; Solomon White,
Bm.

Hughs, Henry & Sally Conger, married 29 Sept. 1859.

Hughs, Jacob E. & May C. Mizell, married 25 Feb. 1861;
David Hughs, Lambert (?) Lawrence, Thomas Alexander, wit.

Hughs, Josiah (X) & Elisabeth Watford, 29 Aug. 1796; James
Hughes, Bm.

Hughs, Miles & Margaret Cowand, 29 Mar. 1862 (lic.). Married 30 Mar. 1862.

Hughs, Whitmell (X) & Elisabeth Layton, 2 Feb. 1808; Allen
(?) Hughes, Bm.

51

Hunt, Malachi & Sarah H. Cooper, 12 May 1823; John W. Cole, Bm.

Hunter, Henry & _____ Harki__, 9 Aug. 1769; Thos. Whitmell, Joseph Bryan, Bm.

Hunter, Job & Martha Hardey, 18 Apr. 1770; Edward Hardy, Bm.

Hunter, Timothy & Synthey Hunter, 11 June 1799; Solomon Cherry, Bm.

Hunter, William & Mary Lewis, 10 May 1796; Hardy Freeman, Bm.

Hurst, William & Sarah Oliver, 22 Nov. 1768; Philip (X) Walston, Bm.

Hyman, Archabald & Frances Volines, 31 Jan. 1859 (lic.). Married 8 Feb. 1859.

Hyman, Hugh & Elizabeth Sparkman, 19 Feb. 1767; Jesse Sparkman, John Reed, Bm.

Hyman, Joel & Polley Pender, 8 Jan. 1800; Solomon Pender, Bm.

Hyman, John & Sarah Smithwick, 20 Feb. 1773; John Moore, Bm.

Hyman, William & Martha Jane Tayloe, 10 Jan. 1853; James W. Smith, Bm. Married 11 Jan. 1853.

Hyman, Wm. C. & Sarah Frances Bowens, 2 Aug. 1849; James (X) Collins, Bm.

Ings, Matthew & Martha Laton, 19 Mar. 1791; John Bittle, Bm.

Jacobs, Samuel & Bethiah Cherrye, 3 Nov. 1788; James Warren, Bm.

Jacobs, Samuel & Happy Sholar, 9 May 1796; George (X) White, Bm.

Jacocks, Charles Worth & Jannett Young, 30 Sept. 1791; Stevens Gray, Bm.; J. Anthony, wit.

Jacocks, Jesse C. (of Perquimons Co.) & Margaret Cotton, married 13 Sept. 1854 by Benjamin S. Bronson, Rector of St. Thomas Church, Windsor, at the house of Mrs. Godwin Cotton.

Jacocks, Jonathan & Elizabeth Hill, _____1790; Henry Hill, Bm.

Jacocks, Jonathan & Elizabeth Hill, 14 Mar. 1791; James Burn, Bm.

BERTIE MARRIAGES, 1762-1868

James, Allen & Nancy Smith, 25 May 1808; Fred R. James, Bm.

James, Andrew (X) & Janey Drury, 24 Feb. 1784; Benjamin (X) James, Bm.

James, Baldy & Mary Sanderlin, married 4 Feb. 1855; Jackson Wilder, Charles Mills, wit.

James, Benjamin (X) & Lucy Murray, 8 Mar. 1779; Christopher (X) Lee, Joel (X) Harrell, Bm.

James, Benjamin (X) & Keziah James, 1 Nov. 1788; John Hicks, Bm.

James, Emanuel & Patience Gardner, 19 Jan. 1788; John Gardner, Bm.

James, Hardy (X) & Mary James, 18 Feb. 1801; Fredrick James, Bm.

James, Haywood & Ruthan Ann Mably, 23 Sept. 1858 (lic.). Married 28 Oct. 1858 at James Mabley's.

James, Moses (X) & Keziah Reed, 3 Aug. 1786; Jeremiah James, Bm.

James, William (X) & Polley Riddle, 4 Sept. 1783; Andrew (X) James, Bm.

James, William & Marina Bartlet, 25 Feb. 1823; Benj. Bartlet, Bm.

Jenkens, L. O. & Jarsey Hollomon, 22 Mar. 1842; Andrew J. Askew, Bm.

Jenkins, Abram & Sally Ann Burden, married 4 Jan. 1855.

Jenkins, Abram & Mary E. Mitchell, married 16 Jan. 1862; Wm. Pritchard, Thos. Swain, Wm. Z. Mitchell, Wm. C. Dunning, Jas. L. Mitchell, Wm. J. Early, wit.

Jenkins, Docton & Rebecca Tadlock, married 11 Mar. 1855; Robert R. Tayloe, Cornelius Huff, Anderson Casper, wit.

Jenkins, Harry & Lucy Jenkins, married 18 Oct. 1868.

Jenkins, John & Marina Godwin, 30 Aug. 1803; Winborn Jenkins, Bm.

Jenkins, John W. & Emily "Emma" Joliff, 17 Jan. 1852; Lodowick (X) Hale, Bm. Married 30 Jan. 1852.

Jenkins, Noah & Elisabeth Harrell, 12 Apr. 1796; Cader (X) Jenkins, Bm.

Jenkins, Robert & Sarah Dunning, married 21 Mar. 1856.

Jenkins, S. W. & Irena Watson, married 22 Oct. 1868.

Jenkins, Samuel & Mary Perry, 15 Dec. 1788; John Perry, Bm.

Jenkins, Wm. P. & Ellen E. Hodges, 30 Oct. 1865 (lic.).
Married 14 Nov. 1865.

Jernigan, Abner & Sarah Jernigan, married 28 Dec. 1856.

Jernigan, Arthur & Mary Bond, 25 Feb. 1790; Benjamin
Jernigan, Bm.

Jernigan, Arthur & Mary Allen, 22 Oct. 1790; Benjamin
Jernigan, Bm.

Jernigan, Burdan & Elizabeth Hoggard, 1 Jan. 1855 (lic.).
Married 4 Jan. 1855.

Jernigan, George & Emily Capehart, married 3 Sept. 1856.

Jernigan, George & Eva Byram, married 20 Jan. 1867.

Jernigan, George & Nancy E. Capehart, married 2 Nov. 1867.

Jernigan, George T. & Martha A. C. Bryant, 9 Jan. 1867
(lic.). Married 10 Jan. 1867.

Jernigan, James (X) & Sarah Pierce, 4 Aug. 1792; Benja.
Jernigan, Bm.

Jernigan, Joseph & Nancy Jernigan, 6 Aug. 1793; Arthur
Jernigan, Bm.

Jernigan, Joseph & Anne Jernigan, 18 Jan. 1794; Ethelred
Jernigan, Bm.

Jernigan, Marcus & Mary Hoggard, 1 Mar. 1853 (lic.). Married 2 Mar. 1853.

Jernigan, William & Pernice Todd, 15 Mar. 1854; Nathaniel
Jernigan, Bm. Married 16 Mar. 1854.

Jinkens, Rigdon & Martha King, 18 Sept. 1798; Richard
Arnold, Bm.

Jinkins, James & Mary Wynn, 11 Jan. 1808; George Wynns, Bm.

Jinkins, Joseph (X) & Mary Meazele, 5 Sept. 1785; James
Mezall, Bm.

Johnson, Harda & Elizabeth Harrison, married 28 May 1866.

Johnson, Haywood & Sarah Castellow, married 15 Mar. 1855.

Johnson, Henry & Harriet Hardy, married 25 Dec. 1866.

Johnson, Henry A. & Jane White, married 30 Jan. 1868.

Johnson, Henry L. & Ann Elizabeth Mizell, 5 July 1865 (lic.). Married 6 July 1865.

Johnson, James P. & Hellen R. Lee, married 1 July 1863.

Johnson, John & Harriet Hoggard, married 21 Aug. 1856.

Johnson, Joseph & Sidney Siscomb, 10 Sept. 1852; Sol Mezel, Bm. Married 16 Sept. 1852.

Johnson, Linyard & Martha E. White, 8 Sept. 1866 (lic.). Married 12 Sept. 1866.

Johnson, Littleton & Susan Ann Hawkins, 27 Sept. 1851; Williamson (X) Rutter, Bm. Married ____1851.

Johnson, Littleton & Sarah E. Kemp, married 29 Jan. 1866.

Johnson, Lot & Peggy Cotton, 17 Sept. 1866 (lic.). Married 22 Sept. 1866.

Johnson, Marcus & Mary Matthias, married 23 Nov. 1854.

Johnson, Marcus R. & Rutha Ann Bird, 20 Dec. 186_ (lic.). Married 21 Dec. 1865.

Johnson, Wheeler & Elizabeth Bird, 17 Mar. 1851; John C. (X) Harrell, Bm. Married 17 Mar. 1851.

Johnston, Alexander Hawkins & Salley Burras, 31 Mar. 1795; Lewis Reddit, Bm.

Johnston, Hardy H. & Temperance Butler, 12 June 1828.

Johnston, Henry & Elizabeth Green, 13 Feb. 1834; William Weston, Bm.

Johnston, Jeremiah & Penny Rogers, 3 Jan. 1803; Thomas Seals, Bm.

Johnston, John & Angelina Cullipher, married 16 Aug. 1860.

Johnston, John W. & Deborah Joiner, married 25 Nov. 1866.

Johnston, John R. & Martha A. Miller, married 19 Jan. 1859.

Johnston, Jonathan & Susan Brayboy, 11 Nov. 1809; Wm. King, Bm.

Johnston, Levy (X) & Mildred Seals, 23 Mar. 1779; John (X) Johnston, John Smith, Bm.

BERTIE MARRIAGES, 1762-1868

Johnston, Luke & Lucretia Barber, 8 Mar. 1831; James C.
Barnacastle, Bm.

Johnston, Thomas (X) & Easter Cullerpher, 1_ Feb. 1784;
Nathaniel (X) Cullipher, Bm.

Johnston, Thomas & (Mrs.) Sarah Knott, 10 Sept. 1787;
Theophilus Redditt, Bm.

Johnston, Thomas & Nancy Outlaw, 4 July 1832; Nathl. Cullipher, Bm.

Johnston, William (X) & Penelope Wynants, 25 Sept. 1804;
Miles Bonner, Bm.

Johnston, William & Mary Niel, 29 Aug. 1829; Ephm. B.
Weston, Bm.

Joiner, Thomas & Francis Cox, married 18 Sept. 1856.

Jones, Albert & Mary Sutton, married 14 Feb. 1867.

Jones, Allen & Elizabeth Holliday, 24 July 1822; Stephen
(X) Allen, Bm.; John W. Harrison, wit.

Jones, Benjamin & Margaret Cox, 5 Jan. 1853; Joseph (X)
_____son, Bm. Married _____.

Jones, Burrel H. & E. C. Veale, 2 June 183_; Thomas J.
Pugh, Jona. S. Tayloe, Bm.

Jones, Dorsey & Celia Harrell, 18 Sept. 1866 (lic.). Married 15 Oct. 1866.

Jones, James (Col.) & Rhoda Barttlett (Col.), married
31 Jan. 1860.

Jones, James C. & Lavinia Brickell, 6 Sept. 1820.

Jones, Jesse (X) & Linah Monk, 21 July 1788; Silas Belote,
Bm.

Jones, Joel & Dicey Harrell, 11 Jan. 1794; David (X) Jones,
Bm.

Jones, John & Elisabeth Duning, 23 Jan. 1798; William (X)
Williford, Bm.

Jones, Sarvent & Temperance Booth (?), 12 Jan. 1782; Cader
Bass, Bm.

Jones, Tony & Rebecca Biggs, married 23 Mar. 1867.

Jones, William & Asia Holliday, 23 Jan. 1790; William H.
(X) Green, Bm.

Jones, William (X) & Anne Dempsey, 18 Dec. 1804; William
(X) Dempsey, Bm.

Jordan, Charles (X) & Penelope Castellaw, 10 Nov. 1792;
George Simons, Bm.

Jordan, Jesse J. & Mary Catharine Clark, married 3 Jan.
1865.

Jordan, Joseph & Martha Jordan, 14 Mar. 1791; Ebenezer
Smithwick, Bm.

Jordan, William & Margaret Clayton, 12 Aug. 1777; William
Williams, Bm.

Jordan, William, Jr. & Mary Jordan, 9 Dec. 1785; Robert
Armistead, Bm.

Josey, Stephen & Nancy Rhodes, 30 Sept. 1805; Whitmell
Rutland, Bm.

Keen, James (X) & Edy Bird, 30 Dec. 1799; Moses Keen, Bm.

Keeter, Charles & Elizabeth Cullipher, married 20 Feb. 1855.

Keeter, George & Elizabeth Johnson, 1 Jan. 1855 (lic.).
Married 3 Jan. 1855.

Keeter, Humphrey & Matilda Pierce, 1 Mar. 1852; William
Keeter, Bm.; W. N. Mitchell, wit. Married 2 Mar. 1852.

Keeter, James & Acenith Pierce, married 31 May 1856.

Keeter, John & Creecy Cullipher, 15 Oct. 1828; John Johnston, Bm.

Keeter, Jonathan & Margaret Grigory, married 14 Mar. 1855.

Keeter, Reuben L. & Sarah E. White, married 19 Jan. 1863.

Keeter, Samuel (X) & Sarah Bowen, 9 Aug. 1796; John Barrett,
Bm.

Keeter, William (X) & Thediah Wilkinson, 8 July 1789; James
(X) Wilkinson, Bm.

Keeter, William (X) & Syntha Phelps, 5 June 1832; Willis
Griffin, Bm.

Keith, William A. & Virginia S. Clary, 16 Nov. 1853; John
Watson, Bm. Married 16 Nov. 1853.

Kelly, William (X) & Mary Burket, 8 Nov. 1780; Alexander
Urquhart, Bm.

Kemp, William A. & Sarah E. Woodard, 6 Dec. 1852 (lic.).
Married 7 Dec. 1852; Zebulon Simmons, George W. McGlaw-
horn, wit.

Kent, Joseph & Rachel Walston, 5 (?) Aug. 1762; Humphrey
Nichols, David Ryan, Bm.

King, Charles & Milley Benton, 12 Dec. 1787; Wm. Gray, Bm.

King, Charles & Elisabeth Benton, 11 July 1796; Elisha
Holden, Bm.

King, David & Sally Ruffin, 18 May 1793; Allen Williams,
Bm.

King, Henry & Sarah Worley, 18 Feb. 1789; Stevens Gray, Bm.

King, Henry, Jr. & Penelope Wimberly, 5 Mar. 1807; William
W. Johnston, Bm.

King, Kadar & Martha House (widow), 10 July 1769; Saml.
Grymes, Bm.

King, Kadar & Mary Skiles, 24 July 1784; John (X) Skiles,
Bm.

King, Michael & Clarisa Worley, 3 Apr. 1793; Henry King,
Bm.

King, Noah & Sarah F. Rascoe, 29 Aug. 1827; Wm. Conley, Bm.

King, Noah & Harriete Weston, 14 Sept. 1853; Benjn. F. King,
Bm. Married 15 Sept. 1853; William Coggin, William Riggsby,
wit.

King, Timothy & Nancy Garrett, 13 Jan. 1820; William King,
Bm.

King, William & Amelia Slade, 28 Nov. 1777; John Johnston,
Bm.; Wm. Benson, wit.

King, William & Abigail Lee, 17 Sept. 1791; Henry Lee, Bm.

Kittrell, Belson & Nancy West, 19 July 1803; Elisha Pender,
Bm.

Kittrell, Demsey & Martha Spivey, 19 June 1777; John Johnston, Bm.

Kittrell, George & Mary Rhodes, 2 Mar. 1793; Jeremiah Leggett, Bm.

Kittrell, Isaac & Elizabeth Reed, 20 Dec. 1805; William
West, Bm.

Kittrell, John & Luisa Kittrell, 10 Apr. 1793; Willis Kittrell, Bm.

Kittrell, John & Mary Lassiter, 19 Apr. 1794; Standley Kittrell, Bm.

Kittrell, John & Polly West, 3 May 1797; Belson Kittrell, Bm.

Kittrell, Standley & Prudence Jordan, 13 Jan. 1799; Benjamin Folks, Bm.

Knott, Absolom & Elisabeth Davidson, 16 Sept. 1779; Luke Collins, Wm. McKenzie, Bm.

Knott, Allin & Rachel Walston, 15 Feb. 1798; William Capehart, Bm.

Knott, John & Priscilla Lawrence, 15 Feb. 1806; Humphrey Lawrence, Bm.

Knott, Joseph (X) & Absaley Mizell, 8 Jan. 1793; James (X) White, Bm.

Knott, Thomas (X) & Frances Cannady, 18 Dec. 1793; James (X) White, Bm.

Lain, David & Celah Askew, __ May 1805; Jesse (X) Barnes, Bm.

Lambertson, Joe & Rose Pool, married 20 Mar. 1866.

Land, John (X) & Sarah Young, 3 Nov. 1775; Thomas Young, Bm.

Lane, Albany & Martha Morris, 16 May 1857 (lic.). Married 17 May 1857.

Lane, John A. P. & Sarah E. Barnacastle, married 1 Jan. 1867.

Lane, Joseph E. & Caroline V. Patrick, 13 Dec. 1852; Wm. J. White, Bm.

Langdale, George & Milley Seawell, 18 May 1832; Joseph (X) Johnston, Bm.

Langdale, John & Lucy Bayly, married 5 June 1866.

Langley, William T. & Mary Shaw, 23 Nov. 1831; Samuel Shaw, Bm.

Laseter, Jesse & Elizabeth Thompson, 31 Jan. 1839; William D. Mitchell, Bm.

Lasky, Thomas & Sarah Stone, 4 Nov. 1786; John Corbert, Bm.

Lasseter, Joseph & Augustus Cooper, married 10 Dec. 1867.

Lassiter, Amos & Sarah Speight, 11 May 1793; Jacob (X) Curry, Bm.

Lassiter, J. F. & L. E. Hawkins, married 13 July 1865.

Lassiter, Jesse & Parthena Early, 11 Dec. 1865 (lic.). Married 19 Dec. 1865.

Lassiter, John & Penelope Rayner, 26 Dec. 1806; John Askew, Bm.

Lassiter, John E. & Rachel Hawkins, married 3 Sept. 1868.

Lassiter, John W. & Phoebee W. Burden, married 3 Dec. 1868.

Laughton, William (X) & Winnefred McDowell, 29 Dec. 1798; Thomas Newborn, Bm.

Laurance, Seth (X) & Betsey Britt, 8 Feb. 1796; John Hicks, Bm.

Laurence, Aquilla & Mary Mason, 1 Jan. 1831; William Langley, Bm.

Laurence, Robert & Elisabeth Cobb, 24 Jan. 1780; Thomas Sutton, Bm.

Laurence, Thomas & Sarah Nichols, 3 Feb. 1784; William Gray, Bm.

Lawrence, Nathaniel P. & Francis Bryan, 31 Jan. 1853; James (X) Dempsey, Bm. Married 2 Feb. 1853.

Lawrence, Robert & Ann Williams, 25 June 1803; Abner Lawrence, Bm.

Lawrence, Thomas & Sarah Ann Hodder, 5 May 1858 (lic.). Married 6 May 1858.

Lawrence, William W. & Elizabeth Davis, married 22 May 1856.

Layton, Alfred & Malinda Morriss, 16 Oct. 1848; John Henry, Bm.

Leary, John & Winefred Garrett, 15 Nov. 1804; William Sparkman, Bm.

Leary, Thomas J. & Elizabeth Gaskins, married 4 Feb. 1857.

Leary, Wm. & Jane Donaldson, married 23 Nov. 1867.

Leatth, Thomas & Elizabeth Wynants, 17 Nov. 1767; Benjamin (X) Cook, Bm.

Ledenham, John (X) & Charlotte _____, 4 Mar. 1789; Amos Harris, Bm.

Lee, Benjamin & Rhoda Mitchell, married 27 Dec. 1866.

Lee, James & Sally Huson, married 16 June 1867.

Lee, John H. & Lavonia Gill, married 2 Feb. 1860.

Lee, Joshua & Fanny King, 10 Oct. 1786; Charles King, Bm.

Lee, Thomas & Lindona Pugh, married 2 Feb. 1867.

Lee, Wm. H. & Emily J. Horn, married 19 Dec. 1865.

Legett, Alexander & Mary Kittrell, 2 Feb. 1788; Thomas Legett, Jeremiah Legett, Bm.

Legett, James & Tabitha Cumi (?) Belote, 11 Oct. 1777; John Legett, Bm.

Legett, James & Mary E. Oxley, 9 Mar. 1850; Joseph White, Bm.

Legett, Nazary & Mary Rascoe, 2 Jan. 1805; Wm. Weston, Bm.

Leggett, Lewis (X) & Ann Hawkins, 3 May 1780; Ephraim (X) Shoulder, Bm.

Leister, James H. & Francis A. Shaw, 25 Sept. 1858 (lic.). Married 26 Sept. 1858.

Lewis, John & (Mrs.) Martha Ryan, _____; George West, Bm.

Lewis, Watson & Anna F. Crutchdow (?), married 25 Mar. 1855.

Lightfoot, John & Elisabeth Rhodes, 4 Sept. 1802; Hardyman Abington, Bm.

Lindsey, Louis & Harriet Askew, 16 Mar. 1866 (lic.). Married 17 Mar. 1866.

Liscombe, William (X) & Sarah Bayley, 27 Sept. 1794; Thomas Calloway, Bm.

Lister, John & Elisabeth Boswell, 22 Apr. 1790; John Weston, Bm.

Liverman, Wm. C. & Adelia R. Peele, married 21 Mar. 1867.

Lloyd, William & Marth_ Cockran, 30 Jan. 1767; Robert Henry, Thomas Jones, Bm.; Frances Hall, wit.

Long, Joel & Mary Long, 29 Jan. 1788; William Long, Bm.

BERTIE MARRIAGES, 1762-1868

Long, Samuel & Sarah Warburton, 21 Aug. 1774; John Irvin (?), Bm.

Love, William & Huldy Hobbs Turnage, 4 Oct. 1794; William Hobbs Turnage, Bm.

Low, John (Col.) & Judy King (Col.), married 25 Dec. 1868.

Lowther, Trestram & Penelope Dawson, 10 Jan. 1786; John Johnston, Bm.

Loyd, Alexander (X) & Margaret Burges, 2 Apr. 1777; Benjamin Forman, Bm.

Loyd, James (X) & Fanny Casper, 7 Feb. 1784; Joseph (X) Loyd, Bm.

Loyd, Josiah (X) & Dolley Cobb, 26 Jan. 1792; William (X) Skiles, Bm.

Luse, Stephen & Nancy Watson, 15 Oct. 1853; Joseph Cooper, Bm. Married 16 Oct. 1853.

Luton, Henry & Martha Cole, 7 Feb. 1831; Powell Bridger, Bm.

Luton, James B. & Angy Elizabeth Collins, married 22 Dec. 1856.

Lynch, James & Alice Cooper, 14 July 1865 (lic.). Married 23 July 1865.

Lyon, John B. & Priscilla A. Pierce, 25 Feb. 1854. Married 2 Mar. 1854; Patrick H. Mountain, John Hoggard, wit.

Maer, Abraham & Prudence Jordan, 15 Sept. 1766; Jas. Campbell, J. P. Jordan, Jun., Bm.; Edmund Blount, Joseph Whedbee, wit.

Maer, Saml. & Margaret Jordan, 3 Apr. 1792; Joseph Jordan, Bm.; Thos. Whitmell Pugh, wit.

Maer, William & Margaret Leggett, 12 July 1803; Thomas Church, Bm.

Maer, Wm. & Mary Rayser, 24 Dec. 1829; W. Blanchard, Bm.

Manly, Alexander & Rebecca Jones, 22 Dec. 1852; Jonas (X) Evans, Bm. Married 23 Dec. 1852; Ryan Butler, William C. Miller, wit.

Manly, King & Nancy Hill, 3 July 1828.

Manning, Hillery & Sarah Lewis, __May 1779; Lemuel Hyman, William Hyman, Bm.

Manning, Luke & Sarah Lawrance, 6 Aug. 1787; John Smithwick, Bm.

Mardra, Joseph & Sarah Smithwick, 26 Dec. 1792; John (X) Madra, Bm.

Mardre, Thomas & Ann Howell, 28 Jan. 1791; Moses Keen, Bm.

Marshall, Samuel & Mary Stone, 26 Dec. 1826; Nazrth. Wilford, Bm.; Jno. W. Bond, wit.

Martin, Jas. B. & Sophia E. Capehart, married 4 Mar. 1868 by Francis W. Hilliard, Rector of St. Paul's Church, Edenton.

Mason, Solomon (X) & Polly Jones, 25 Sept. 1797; Micajah (X) Wilks, Bm.

Massengale, Kinchen & Elenor Dwyer, 31 Dec. 1801; Danl. Massgale, Bm.

Matthews, Jacob & Amillia Bazemore, married 22 May 1866.

Matthews, James A. & Mary E. Mitchell, married 5 July 1860.

McCaskey, John & Mary Razer, 29 Jan. 1767; Edward Rasor, Bm.

McClee, James & Elizabeth White, 29 Dec. 1804; John Daren, Bm.

McClellan, William (X) & Sally Hallom, 15 May 1795; Josiah (X) Harrell, Bm.

McClure, Solomon & Margaret Bond, 26 Dec. 1866 (lic.).

McCottor, John & Elizabeth Benson, 8 Aug. 1805; Wm. Montgomery, Bm.

McDaniel, Jas. (X) & Opaliza Dempsey, 30 Aug. 1849; Jona. S. Tayloe, Bm.

McDowall, John & Temperance Jinkins, 8 Dec. 1795; George Andrews, Bm.

McDowell, Miles & Elisabeth Holley, 29 May 1797; Jacob (X) Outlaw, Bm.

McGlaehan, Hardy (X) & Anne Gaskins, 22 Mar. 1792; Robert Hunter, Bm.

McGlauehan, Jeremiah (X) & Elisabeth Capehart, 23 Apr. 1803; John (X) Allum, Bm.

McGlauhon, Jeremiah (X) & Nancy Baker, 26 Jan. 1805; Ruben (X) Harreson, Bm.

BERTIE MARRIAGES, 1762-1868

McGlauhon, William & Ann Gaskin, 11 Jan. 1780; John Oxley, Bm.

McGlauhon, Wm. F. & Julia Ann White, married 5 Sept. 1855.

McKinzy, James & Martha Turner, 17 Apr. 1787; William Turner, Bm.; Thos. Ryan Butler, wit.

McWell, James & Sarah Redditt, 12 Feb. 1807; Hardy Oxley, Bm.

Mebane, Wm. & Mary Ashburn, __ Feb. 1852; Jno. W. Bond, Bm.

Mebane, William A. & Margaret M. Bond, married 15 Mar. 1866.

Melone, Drury & Frances Bentley; 19 July 1788; Noah Belote, Bm.

Melton, Weston & Rebecca Ward, married 13 Jan. 1854.

Merideth, Davis & Rachel Farror, 4 Feb. 1791; Richard Billups, Bm.

Merritt, Daniel & Emiline Pugh, married 26 Dec. 1867.

Miears, Nathan & Elizabeth Outlaw, 15 Sept. 1764; Titus Edwards, Bm.

Miers, George & Elizabeth Kale, 15 Feb. 1827; Lawrence Horne (?), Bm.

Miers, Samuel (X) & Christian Cobb, 27 Dec. 1800; Thos. Mitchell, Bm.

Milburn, Alexander & Sarah Pedin, 9 Mar. 1799; William Spivey, Bm.

Milburn, Arnold C. & Raney Harrell, 4 Feb. 1800; Joshua (X) Harrell, Bm.

Milburn, Henry Clay & Martha "Patsey" Whitfield, 26 July 1796; Henry Flury, Bm.

Miller, Benjamin (X) & Martha Cullifer, 3 Sept. 1804; Thos. Teal, Bm.

Miller, Elisha & Harriette Bunch, 14 Feb. 1853; J. F. Britton, Bm.

Miller, Ephraim & Elizabeth King, 28 Apr. 1791; Richard Dawson, Bm.

Miller, Ephraim & Mary Brimage, 9 Sept. 1795; William Sutton, Bm.

Miller, Harrell (X) & Sylvia Ann Brown, 30 May 1853 (lic.). Married 31 May 1853.

64

BERTIE MARRIAGES, 1762-1868

Miller, Jesse & Martha Todd, married 3 Apr. 1860.

Miller, John & Clary Misell, 22 Feb. 1806; Reuben Mellon, Bm.

Miller, John (X) & Penny Ray, 31 Jan. 1821; William Mizells, Bm.

Miller, John H. & Francis Todd, married 25 Nov. 1855.

Miller, Jonathan & Sarah Jane Brown, married 21 Mar. 1867.

Miller, Josiah & Martha Brantley, 24 Mar. 1853; Salamer Miller, Bm. Married 28 Mar. 1853.

Miller, Josiah & Mary Ann White, married 15 Oct. 1868.

Miller, Levi & Julia A. McFarland, married 20 Dec. 1860.

Miller, Lewis & Margaret Meazle, 25 Jan. 1808; Reuben Miller, Bm.

Miller, Reddick & Martha Mansfield, 15 Nov. 1832; William W. Cherry, Bm.

Miller, Reuben & Sarah Misells, 23 Dec. 1799; Lewis Miller, Bm.

Miller, Solomon & Mary Harrill, 25 Apr. 1852; John L. Butler, Bm.

Miller, Wm. & Jane Mizells, married 1 Oct. 1856.

Miller, Wm. R. C. W. & Nancy A. Miller, 12 Dec. 1866 (lic.). Married 13 Dec. 1866.

Mills, Charles & Jane Ash, 26 May 1853; John (X) Snow, Bm. Married 26 May 1853; William N. Mitchell, wit.

Milton, Weston & Rebecca Ward, 13 Jan. 1854; Dickison (X) Milton, Bm.

Minard, John (X) & Sarah Baker, 29 Jan. 1795; Levy Baker, Bm.

Minton, Benjamin & Olive Reed, 15 Feb. 1790; Robert Bridger, Jr., Bm.

Minton, David H. & Mary E. Powell, 24 Nov. 1866 (lic.). Married 27 Nov. 1866.

Minton, J. Madison & Magt. Jane Morgan, 24 Dec. 1850; George (X) Jenkins, Bm.

Minton, James & Margaret Modlin, married 26 Dec. 1850.

65

BERTIE MARRIAGES, 1762-1868

Minton, Jas. & M. I. White, married 20 Mar. 1866.

Minton, Thomas & Catherine Harrell, married 10 July 1856.

Minton, Thos. & Sally Jones, married 18 May 1858; Benja.
Jones, Benja. Cook, wit.

Mires, David (X) & Sarah Peton, 17 July 1803; Alexander
Milburn, Bm.

Mires, Elisha Bird (X) & Polly Barrot, 5 Apr. 1796; John
Standley, Bm.

Mires, Nathan (X) & Winnefred Morris, 30 Sept. 1800; John
Morriss, Bm.

Mires, Nathan (X) & Polly White, 22 July 1809; Jesse (X)
Hoggard, Bm.; Baldy Ashburn, wit.

Mitchel, Joseph (X) & Sarah Williams, 30 Dec. 1779; Zekial
(X) Mitchel, Bm.

Mitchell, Abram & Perlina Cherry, married 20 May 1866.

Mitchell, Bryant & Martha Todd, 23 Jan. 1854; Gaven H.
Mitchell, Bm. Married 24 Jan. 1854.

Mitchell, Elisha & Elisabeth Holley, 31 Dec. 1796; Nathan
(X) Cobb, Bm.

Mitchell, George (X) & Aggy Holder, 20 Dec. 1830.

Mitchell, Grandison M. & Leora C. Joliff, married 8 July
1862.

Mitchell, Henry & Rose Askew, married 20 Aug. 1865.

Mitchell, Henry & Harriet Hays, married 10 Jan. 1866.

Mitchell, Henry C. & Ann J. Miller, married 5 Feb. 1867.

Mitchell, (Dr.) Henry S. & Mary J. Burden, 10 Nov. 1852;
Wm. D. Mitchell, Bm. Married 11 Nov. 1852; Shadrach M.
Moore, Wm. D. Mitchell, wit.

Mitchell, James H. & Elizabeth E. White, married 24 Dec.
1860.

Mitchell, James L. S. & Frances Gilliam, 15 Oct. 1851; L.
J. Webb, Bm. married 21 Oct. 1851.

Mitchell, Jeremiah & Sarah Morriss, 4 Dec. 1832; Wm. W.
Cherry, Bm.

Mitchell, Jeremiah & Mary Elizabeth Williams, married 5
Aug. 1866.

BERTIE MARRIAGES, 1762-1868

Mitchell, Jeremiah & Peggy Butler, married 17 Jan. 1867.

Mitchell, John & Elisabeth Farmer, 12 Nov. 1799; Elisha
Brinkley, Bm.

Mitchell, John A. & Martha Taylor, married 3 Oct. 1859.

Mitchell, John H. (X) & Martha Mitchell, 26 Mar. 1852.
Married 30 Mar. 1852; William Holloman, Perry Mitchell,
Josiah Mitchell, wit.

Mitchell, John H. & Priscilla Burdan, married 16 Jan. 1868.

Mitchell, Jonas (X) & Margaret Standley, 19 Aug. 1794;
Jonathan Spivey, Bm.

Mitchell, Jos. & Temperance Ann Donaldson, married 18 Aug.
1857.

Mitchell, Joseph J. & Jarsey Ann Williams, married 23 Sept.
1866.

Mitchell, Kants & Harriet Freeman, married 25 Dec. 1868.

Mitchell, Kenny & Rose Askew, married 20 Aug. 1865.

Mitchell, William & Renney Nicoles (?), 11 July 1802; John
Williford, Bm.

Mitchell, Wm. D. & Phoebe E. Burdan, married 4 Mar. 1862;
Wm. Spivey, Calvin Pritchard, James Burdan, Abram Jenkins,
Edward Morris, wit.

Mitchell, Wm. J. & Sarah A. M. Byram, married 11 Jan. 1866.

Mitchell, William W. & Martha Williford, 1 Oct. 1832.

Mitchell, William W. & Martha E. Mitchell, 15 June 1834;
Wright Mitchell, Bm.

Mitchell, Wright & Martha Ann Outlaw, 19 Dec. 1827.

Mitchell, Zadock & Mary Jinkins, 31 Dec. 1799; William
Mitchell, Bm.

Mitchell, Zadok D. & Balinda Burden, 25 Jan. 1848; Jona.
S. Tayloe, Bm.

Mizell, Aaron & Polly Quall (?), 28 Dec. 1802; Timothy
Mizell, Bm.

Mizell, Aaron & Mary Boswell, married 24 Oct. 1867.

Mizell, Cader (X) & Mary Hare, 8 Oct. 1783; Soloman Millar,
Bm.

BERTIE MARRIAGES, 1762-1868

Mizell, Charles & Ann Rebecca Butler, married 6 Dec. 1866.

Mizell, David & Elizabeth Waller, 23 May 1857 (lic.). Married 24 May 1857; (Dr.) Stark Smith, Thos. Fannin, Robert White, wit.

Mizell, George & Nancy Gaskins, 22 Jan. 1828; Aaron Mizell, Bm.

Mizell, Henry C. & Mary Ward, 26 Nov. 1851; Geo. (X) Mitchell, Bm. Married 26 Nov. 1851.

Mizell, Hezekiah & Nancy Britain, __ May 1805; Solo. Cherry, Junr., Bm.

Mizell, Isaac & Charlett Hughes, 19 Feb. 1799; George (X) Hughes, Bm.

Mizell, Jeremiah & Winefred Sowell, 11 Mar. 1807; Reuban Millan, Bm.

Mizell, John & Winnefred Miller, 9 Nov. 1789; Timothy Mizell, Bm.

Mizell, John & Mary Mitchel, 8 Jan. 1791; Reuben (X) Harrison, Bm.

Mizell, John & Martha Morris, 13 Mar. 1802; Matthew Morriss, Bm.

Mizell, John D. & Eliza White, married 15 Apr. 1862.

Mizell, Jonas (X) & Patty Widid (?), 29 Jan. 1784; Joseph (X) Morriss, Bm.

Mizell, Joseph & Frances Lary, 22 Mar. 1791; John Mizell, Bm.

Mizell, Moses & Mary Layton, 6 Mar. 1799; Zadock Moriss, Bm.

Mizell, Solomon & Winnifred Keeter, 24 July 1865 (lic.). Married 25 July 1865.

Mizell, Thomas (X) & Catharine Knott, 16 Feb. 1785; James Langton, Bm.

Mizell, Washington (Col.) & Hester Cooper, married 8 Nov. 1868; J. J. Jacocks, wit.

Mizell, William & Winefred Ward, 10 Nov. 1806; Lewis Miller, Bm.

Mizell, William & Rachel Sackey, 13 Nov. 1833.

Mizell, Wm. (X) & Margt. A. Jacobs, 9 May 1849; John Freeman, Jn. B. Cherry, Wm. S. Pruden, H. A. Gilliam, Bm.

Mizelle, Haywood (Col.) & Emiline Holley (Col.), married
31 Oct. 1868.

Mizells, Augustus & Eliza. Morriss, 16 Dec. 1851; William
(X) Collins, Bm. Married 18 Dec. 1851.

Mizells, Charles & Winnifred Thomas, married 12 Nov. 1855;
Wm. Hoggard, John Mizells, wit.

Mizells, Eli T. & Adaline White, 10 Apr. 1860 (lic.). Married 11 Apr. 1860.

Mizells, Henry & Elizabeth J. Jernigan, 15 Feb. 1860 (lic.).
Married 16 Feb. 1860.

Mizells, Jeremiah & Elizabeth Gray, married 22 Nov. 1855;
James H. Cherry, Robert White, wit.

Mizells, John & Martha Todd, 13 Dec. 1796; Hardy Todd, Bm.

Mizells, Joseph G. & Nancy Mizells, married 28 Nov. 1865.

Mizells, Miles & Elizabeth Simons, married 7 Jan. 1868.

Mizells, Thomas & Feribe Brown, 7 Feb. 1850; Joseph Oder,
Bm.

Mizells, Thomas T. & Ritta Harrison, married 17 Feb. 1859;
David L. Simons, Alonzo Asbill, wit.

Mizells, Timothy & Martha A. Miller, 5 May 1854; Sol.
Mizel, Bm. Married 4 May 1854.(sic)

Mizells, William & Emily Wiggins, 14 Dec. 1853; Alexander
(X) Nixon, Bm. Married 15 Dec. 1853.

Mizles, Isaac & Nancy Thomas, 10 Mar. 1827; William (X)
Mitchel, Bm.

Modlin, Nathan & Elizabeth Outlaw, 22 Aug. 1805; Solomon
White, Bm.

Mohun, Joel & Mary Ashburn, 8 Sept. 1800; William Lee Gray,
Bm.

Monk, Thomas & Frances West, 3 Mar. 1801; Thomas Spence,
Bm.

Monk, Thomas & Anna Swain, 24 Nov. 1808; John Rhodes, Bm.

Moore, Benjamin & Elizabeth Forest, ___ Apr. 1775; Thomas
Harrison, Bm.

Moore, Benton K. & Martha Peele, 28 Jan. 1840; John Freeman, Bm.

Moore, Charles J. & Sarah Frances Yates, married 16 Dec. 1863.

Moore, David & Clarissa Morris, 1 Jan. 1866 (lic.). Married 14 Jan. 1866.

Moore, James & Deborough Clayton, 15 Sept. 1774; William Jordan, Jun., Maurice Moore, Bm.; Martin Griffin, John Smithwick, wit.

Moore, James W. (of Hertford Co.) & Henrietta Raby, married 24 Apr. 1856.

Moore, Jeremiah & Margaret West, 27 Jan. 1807; Sam Howell, Bm.

Moore, Joseph & Priscilla Atkinson, 29 Oct. 1790; Alexr. Frazier, Bm.

Moore, Joseph & Mary Sowell, 1 Dec. 1794; David Tayloe, Bm.

Moore, Lawrence & Bitha Moore, 12 Feb. 1798; Langley Granbery, Bm.

Moore, Moses & Penney Rhodes, 20 May 1803; Benjamin Coffield, Bm.

Moore, Shadrick & Winafred Bunch, 18 Nov. 1830; J. S. Tayloe, William Hendrixen, Bm.

Moore, Titus & Sarah Turner, 3 July 1792; Geo. House, Bm.

Moore, William & Penelope Cannady, 19 Aug. 1793; William Weston, Bm.

Morgan, Seth (X) & Delilah Smith, 19 Jan. 1820; Hary Phelps, Bm.

Morgan, Seth & Affa Curry, 11 June 1827; Charles Cobb, Bm.

Morris, Abraham & Elisabeth Mitchel, 13 Jan. 1785; William Smith, Bm.

Morris, Alpheus & Christian E. Thompson, married 1 Jan. 1857.

Morris, Benjamin & Adaline Outlaw, married 4 Aug. 1866.

Morris, Edward & Ann Mariah Augustus Miers, 8 Aug. 1853; W. T. Sharrock, Bm. Married 11 Aug. 1853; Whitmill T. Sharrack, Alden Bazemore, Joseph Morris, wit.

Morris, Edward S. & Arabella Henry, married 16 Jan. 1868.

Morris, Eli & Elizer Wiggins, married 30 Jan. 1856.

Morris, Elijah (X) & Sarah Green, 22 Dec. 1802; James Keen, Bm.

Morris, Gabriel & Rebecca Jones, married 16 Aug. 1855.

Morris, George & Caroline Perry, 14 Oct. 1865 (lic.). Married 15 Oct. 1865.

Morris, George & Winny Harman, married 28 Feb. 1867.

Morris, Joseph & Mary E. Willoughby, 22 May 1851; John Rice, Bm. Married 22 May 1851.

Morris, Joseph & Nancy Freeman, married 9 Jan. 1867.

Morris, Nathan (Col.) & Betty Ward (Col.), 24 Dec. 1867 (lic.). Married 25 Dec. 1867.

Morris, William & Mary Miller, 20 Apr. 1798; Moses Keen, Bm.

Morris, William T. & Sarah Freeman, married 26 Aug. 1868.

Morris, Zadock & Martha Ann Outlaw, married 3 Oct. 1855.

Morriss, Abraham & Penelope Smith, 8 Aug. 1797; Asa (X) Early, Bm.

Morriss, Calvin J. & Bettie A. Northcott, married 17 Dec. 1868.

Morriss, Edward & Mary Parker, 13 Mar. 1848; Enoch (X) Simpson, Bm.

Morriss, Jacob & Penelope Baker, 24 Oct. 1803; Moses Morriss, Bm.

Morriss, James & Loving Britt, 7 Nov. 1791; Nottingham Monk, Bm.

Morriss, James & Tempy Willoughby, 7 Sept. 1821; John Willoughby, Bm.

Morriss, James & Catherine Harrell, __ ____ 183_; Jesse (X) Harrell, Jr., Bm.

Morriss, Matthew (X) & Penelope Morgan, 10 Jan. 1797; Jonas Bowls, Bm.

Morriss, Matthew & Dicey Outlaw, 20 Dec. 1804; John Mizell, Bm.

Morriss, Matthew & Penelope Jernigan, 23 Mar. 1827; Wm. Watford, Bm.

Morriss, Moses & Elisabeth Yearley, 5 Sept. 1796; Wright Williford, Bm.

Morriss, Thomas (Col.) & M. Holley (Col.), married 25 Oct. 1868.

Morriss, William & Rhodea Mitchel, 22 Nov. 1790; John (X) Mitchel, Bm.

Morriss, William (X) & Sarah Pilont, 29 Nov. 1792; John Wolfenden, Bm.

Morriss, William & Cene Butler, 13 Dec. 1865 (lic.). Married 14 Dec. 1865.

Mullen, Greenbery & Harriot Walston, 27 Mar. 1802; William Brogdon, Bm.

Mullin, Thomas & Fanney Pirkens, 2 Feb. 1786; John Hunter, Bm.

Murdagh, John & Julia Baker, 25 July 1806; John Hodges, Bm.

Myers, George & Priscilla Rice, married 10 Jan. 1856.

Myers, J. J. & Catharine Williams, 10 Nov. 1866 (lic.). Married 11 Nov. 1866.

Myers, Moses (X) & Winefred Watford, 4 Jan. 1804; Nathan (X) Mires, Bm.

Myers, Nathan & Sally Ann Askew, married 10 Jan. 1867.

Myrick, Joshua W. & Temperance A. R. Tyler, 5 Jan. 1833; C. C. Tyler, Bm.

Newbern, Henderson & Sally Hughes, married 26 Apr. 1866.

Newbern, John & Martha A. R. Coffield, married 3 Sept. 1868.

Newborn, Thomas & Elizabeth Sparkman, 7 Oct. 1788; Joseph Mizell, Bm.

Newby, William & Mary Elizer Jordan, married 25 Aug. 1867.

Newcomb, Jesse & Martha Clifton, 24 Feb. 1795; James Clifton, Bm.

Newsom, David A. & Mary Ann Carter, married 23 Feb. 1860.

Niblet, Robert & Georgianna Bowden, married 17 Jan. 1856.

Nicholls, John & Elizabeth Williams, 12 Sept. 1793.

Nicholls, Joseph H. & Celia Howard, married 23 May 1855; Warren Peele, Reddick Howard, wit.

Nicholls, Thomas & Elizabeth Peele, married __ ____ 1856.

Nichols, Noah & Sarah Earley, 20 Oct. 1798; Wright Williford, Bm.

Nixon, John E. & Lucinda J. Mizell, married 8 Mar. 1868.

Nixon, Richard & Ann Jacocks, 24 May 1793; Jonathan Jacocks, Bm.

Nixon, Wm. L. & Lucy A. Simmons, married 15 Mar. 1866.

Norfleet, Aaron & Venus Veale, married 19 May 1866.

Norfleet, Ben & Harriet Wilkins, married 10 Mar. 1866.

Norfleet, James & Elisabeth Hayes, 14 Nov. 1797; Edward Acree, Bm.

Norfleet, Stephen A. & Frances Pugh, 13 June 1849 (lic.).

Norman, Nathan D. & Deborah Heckstall, 5 Sept. 1852; William A. Keith, Bm.; Wm. N. Mitchell, wit. Married 5 Sept. 1852.

Northcut, Wm. T. & Octavia Rayner, 18 Nov. 1865 (lic.). Married 19 Nov. 1865.

Nowell, Alpheus & Virginia A. Britton, 30 Nov. 1858 (lic.). Married 22 Dec. 1858.

Nowell, Joseph & Sally Miller, married 30 Jan. 1855.

Nowell, Rian & Penny Bazemore, married 6 Jan. 1867.

Nowell, Wm. & Eveline Evans, married 13 June 1859.

Nusome, James (X) & Susanna Ward, 7 Aug. 1792; Jacob Garrett, Bm.

Oder, Joseph & Elizabeth Hodder, 20 Nov. 1850; Wm. (X) Oder, Bm.

Oder, Reuben L. & Fanny W. Ray, 4 Mar. 1863 (lic.) Married 5 Mar. 1863.

Oder, William A. & Rebecca Craddoc, married 19 Dec. 1861.

Odom, Richard B. & Anthony V. Williams, married 24 June 1866 (?).

Oliver, Andrew & Maryann West, 30 Jan. 1769; William West, Bm.

Oliver, John, Jr. & Milley Watsford, 27 Feb. 1788; John Oliver, Bm.

Oliver, Malachi & Polly Edwards, 29 Apr. 1798; James Thomas, Bm.

Oliver, Martin & Happy Mitchel, 7 Dec. 1791; John Oliver, Bm.

O'Neil, Charles & Mary Halsey, 9 Nov. 1802; John W. Castellaw, Bm.

Outlaw, David & Martha Standley, 27 July 1773; George Outlaw, Bm.

Outlaw, David & Anne Watford, 23 Dec. 1801; Morgan Outlaw, Bm.

Outlaw, David & Mary Powell, 10 July 1805; Wm. H. Green, Bm.

Outlaw, Edward (son of Edward Outlaw, Jr.) & Lucy Rascoe, married 10 Nov. 1868.

Outlaw, George & Agnis Knott, 19 Mar. 1775; David Outlaw, Bm.

Outlaw, George & Fanny Belote, 27 May 1803; William Outlaw, Bm.

Outlaw, George, Jr. & Marry Askew, 8 ____ 1809; Thomas (X) Cherry, Bm.

Outlaw, George W. & Sally Ann Cherry, married 30 Jan. 1867.

Outlaw, Joshua & Rachel Alexander, 26 Mar. 1805; John Sowell (?), Bm.

Outlaw, Ralph & Mary Knott (widow), 29 Apr. 1769; Peter Clifton, David Outlaw, Bm.

Outlaw, Ralph (X) & Celia Mitchell, 5 Aug. 1808; Nathan Modlin, Bm.

Outlaw, William & Susannah Bird, 25 Aug. 1764; Josiah Stallings, Bm.

Outlaw, William (X) & Rachel Floyd, 5 Apr. 1800; Arthur Pinner, Bm.; Needham Jarnagan, wit.

Outlaw, William J. & Elleanor Outlaw, 22 May 1858 (lic.). Married 27 May 1858.

Overton, Asa & Patsey Tart, 26 Dec. 1789; James Tart, Bm.

Overton, James (X) & Milley Mitchell, 26 Nov. 1788; John (X) Thomas, Bm.

Overton, James T. & Patience Ray, 2 Aug. 1794; John Pender, Bm.

Owens, John (X) & Milley Rasior, 29 Sept. 1800; William Smithwick, Bm.

Owens, Timothy & Ritta Cullipher, 3 Apr. 1834; William Simons, Bm.

Oxley, John, Junr. & Fanny Shoulders, 10 Dec. 1799; Aaron Freeman, Bm.

Oxley, John Hardy & Harritte Lawrence, 28 June 1853; James (X) Leggett, Bm. Married 29 June 1853.

Oxly, Hardy & Sarah McGlauhon, 12 Feb. 180_; Will Copeland, Bm.

Pace, Samuel & Agatha Owens, 10 Jan. 1780; Elisha Rhodes, Bm.

Page, Joshua (X) & Elizabeth Montgomery, 9 Oct. 1787; Jesse (X) Bryan, Bm.

Page, Nathan (X) & Delina Owens, 28 July 1798; James Jordan, Bm.; Elisabeth Bryan, wit.

Page, Solomon (X) & Sarah Hayse, 16 May 1786; John Dodrill, Bm.; Thos. Ryan Butes (?), wit.

Page, Solomon & Saly Holland, 20 Apr. 1830; Joshua M. Page, Bm.

Page, Thomas & Elizabeth Averit, 21 Sept. 1778; George Wair, Bm.

Parker, Abraham (X) & Elizabeth Baker, 13 July 1824; Daniel Powell, Bm.

Parker, Daniel & Patsey Johnston, 30 Dec. 1805; Wm. Sowell, Bm.

Parker, Elisha (X) & Patience Hodge, 16 Jan. 1793; Luke (X) Parker, Bm.

Parker, Francis & Rachel Holland, 19 Oct. 1795; Sewell Holland, Bm.

Parker, George & Sally Cooper, married 2 Apr. 1856.

Parker, Grandison P. & Mary M. Howard, married 4 July 1866.

Parker, Isaac & Ellen Hall, married 2 Mar. 1867.

Parker, John (X) & Parthena Baker, 12 ____ 1808; Elisha
(X) Parker, Bm.

Parker, John & Elizabeth Turner, 18 Jan. 1848.

Parker, John B. & Martha Barnes, married 30 Oct. 1856.

Parker, Jordan & Jarsey C. Morris, married 6 Jan. 1858;
Jos. G. Willoughby, wit.

Parker, Luke (X) & Anne Pierce, 7 Nov. 1794; Reuben (X)
Parker, Bm.

Parker, Nazareth W. & Sarah Hall, 11 Aug. 1866 (lic.).
Married 22 Aug. 1866.

Parker, Reuben & Barbara King, 15 Aug. 1806; Hypy. Smithwick, Bm.

Parker, Richard & Elisabeth King, 7 Oct. 1780; Michael
King, Bm.

Parker, Robert A. & Ann E. Rayner, 20 May 1852; D. E.
Tayloe, Bm. Married 20 May 1852; S. B. Smith, George
Gray, wit.

Parker, Wm. (X) & Elizabeth Lewis, 3 Mar. 1821; Elisha
(X) Parker, Bm.

Patterson, James (of Granville Co.) & Clairacy Bustin
(of Halifax Co.) "These persons wish to get married
and want license for the same."

Patterson, Moses & Marina Smith, 4 Dec. 1823; Godwin Cotten, Bm.

Patterson, William D. & Mary Byram, 17 July 1857 (lic.).
Married 19 July 1857.

Peale, Amos & Nancy Davison, 14 Feb. 1828; Edw. A. Hardy,
Bm.

Peale, Exum & Rhody Harrell, 8 Nov. 1804; Samuel (X) Job,
Bm.

Peale, Jonas (X) & Mary Davison, 30 Nov. 1803; William
McFarlane, Bm.

Pearce, Matthew & Frances Lawrence, 27 Nov. 1806; David
Lawrence, Bm.

Pearce, Thomas & Morning Bryan, 8 Oct. 1791; John Bond, Bm.

Pearce, William & Polly Keane, 19 Dec. 1805; Richd. Keane, Bm.

Peele (?), Calvin & Mary N. Harrell, married 14 Nov. 1867.

Peele, Charles & Jane Moore, married 20 Dec. 1866.

Peele, Drew & Sinna Pritchard, 28 Dec. 1853; James Peeele, Bm. Married 29 Dec. 1853.

Peele, Exum & Elizabeth Wilkes, 3 May 1831; Jonas (X) Gray, Bm.

Peele, Hezekiah (X) & Barbara Cullen, 25 Oct. 1809; Sterling (X) Frances, Bm.

Peele, James & Harriet Acre, 17 Dec. 1827.

Peele, James W. & Elizabeth W. Rawles, married 18 Jan. 1866.

Peele, John & Renney Harrell, 23 Aug. 1794; Jacob Higgs, Bm.

Peele, Richard & Sarah Cook, 6 Mar. 1852; R. H. Cox, Bm. Married 4 Apr. 1852.

Peele, Thomas & Francis Acre, 14 Feb. 1853; W. J. Cox, Bm. Married 17 Feb. 1853.

Peele, William & Lucy Rhodes, 11 Aug. 1800; Reuben Hughs, Bm.

Peele, William E. & Laura A. Acre, married 26 July 1868.

Pender, John & Elizabeth Hubbord, 15 Oct. 1795; William Griffin, Bm.

Pender, Joseph & Rachel Emily Thomas, married 2 June 1867.

Pender, Reddick & Nanny Hambleton, 4 June 1827; William Hambleton, Bm.

Pender, Stephen & Mary Lambert, 8 Jan. 1807; Wm. Sowell, Bm.

Pender, Thomas & Mary Gilman, 25 May 1777; John Johnston, Bm.

Pender, William & Ann Hubbard, 22 Sept. 1800; Belson Kittrell, Bm.

Penny, James & Polly Folk, 23 Aug. 1805; Jno. H. Pugh (?), Bm.

Percie, Zadock (X) & Elisabeth Asbell, 9 Oct. 1792; Joseph (X) Harrell, Bm.

Perry, C. H. (Col.) & Mary Holley, married 21 Nov. 1868.

Perry, Etherton & Emiline Outlaw, married 17 Aug. 1859.

Perry, Freeman & Harriet Ann Perry, married 6 Feb. 1868.

Perry, Gervis P. & Mary Hughs, married 18 Dec. 1856.

Perry, James & Sarah Parker, 7 June 1809; Freeman Perry, Bm.

Perry, John W. & Mary Ann Perry, married 6 Nov. 1861.

Perry, Joseph & Sally E. Cobb, 1 Jan. 1851; H. J. Britt, Bm. Married _____.

Perry, Joseph J. & Temperance J. Perry, 19 Feb. 1856 (lic.). Married 20 Feb. 1856.

Perry, Lewis D. & Judy C. Outlaw, married 3 June 1858; Wm. G. Marsh, Benjn. White, Jos. B. Holloman, wit.

Perry, M. W. & Salley J. Perry, 19 July 1865 (lic.). Married 23 July 1865.

Perry, Thomas & Martha Perry, 6 Mar. 1851; Martin (X) Perry, Bm.

Perry, William & Mary Baker, married 8 Feb. 1858.

Perry, Wright (X) & Kiddy Morriss, 10 Mar. 1830; Jeremiah Outlaw, Bm.

Persey, William (X) & Elisabeth Pearce, 25 Aug. 1785; John Persey, Bm.

Phelps, Abram & Sarah Butler, 13 May 1834; Thomas Bazemore, Bm.

Phelps, Charles & Caroline Castellow, married 28 Oct. 1856.

Phelps, Elisha & Eunice Butler, 7 Sept. 1852; Charles T. (X) Jenkins, Bm. Married 8 Sept. 1852; Joseph Jenkins, Milton Downs, Andrew J. Dunning, wit.

Phelps, George & Martha Williams, married 13 Oct. 1867.

Phelps, Hary & Martha Brown, 19 Jan. 1820; Seth (X) Morgan, Bm.

Phelps, Henry P. & Margaret P. Shaw, married 7 June 1866.

Phelps, Jesse & Casanda Cullipher, married 16 Dec. 1858.

Phelps, John A. & Ritta Boswell, married 11 Aug. 1859.

Phelps, John Wm. & Martha Catharine Davidson, 26 Dec. 1865 (lic.). Married 28 Dec. 1865.

Phelps, John W. & Penelope Pierce, married 15 Sept. 1866.

Phelps, Joseph & Christian Castellow, married 28 Dec. 1855.

Phelps, W. T. & Casandra Phelps, married 15 July 1868.

Phelps, Wm. T. & Susan A. Phelps, 3 Mar. 1866 (lic.). Married 4 Mar. 1866.

Pierce, Abington & Harriet Cullipher, 22 Dec. 1830.

Pierce, David & Lucretia Thompson, 27 Dec. 1854 (lic.). Married 28 Dec. 1854.

Pierce, David & Crissey Cobb, 11 Dec. 1865 (lic.). Married 14 Dec. 1865.

Pierce, Isaac & Mary Jane Grigory, 5 Oct. 1866 (lic.). Married 11 Oct. 1866.

Pierce, James & Mary Hodges, 23 Nov. 1795; William Hodges, Bm.

Pierce, James Richard & Sally Cherry Perry, 17 Oct. 1866 (lic.). Married 18 Oct. 1866.

Pierce, John W. & Harriet Ann Perry, married 7 Feb. 1867.

Pierce, Lodawick & Easther E. Askew, 24 Dec. 1866 (lic.). Married 27 Dec. 1866.

Pierce, Quinton T. & Margaret J. Pierce, married 5 July 1866.

Pierce, Richardson & Susan Ward, 28 Oct. 1857 (lic.). Married 29 Oct. 1857.

Pierce, Turner & Ann Garrett, 19 Dec. 1832; John Moore, Bm.

Pierce, William & Polly Hardin, 15 Aug. 1806; Mathew (X) Pearce, Bm.

Pierce, William & Frances Whitley, 1 May 1834; David (X) Brown, Bm.

Pierce, William H. & Sally Barnacastle, married 6 Dec. 1866; Eli Mizells, William D. Hardin, wit.

Pierce, William R. & Clarissa L. South, 20 Aug. 1866 (lic.). Married 23 Aug. 1866.

Pilant, Enoch & Polly Minton, 8 Mar. 1828.

Pittman, Edward D. & Ann Bunch, 20 Dec. 1858 (lic.). Married 24 Dec. 1859.(sic)

BERTIE MARRIAGES, 1762-1868

Plummer, Armistead (Col.) & Susan Ann Armistead (Col.)
(dau. of George Armistead), 3 Dec. 1867 (lic.). Married
4 Dec. 1867; George Armistead, Andrew Boldin, Gefson
Capehearte, wit.

Plummer, Wm. & Elizer Armistead, 18 June 1821; F. R. Lloyd,
Bm.

Pollock, Jacob & Sarah Thompson, 1 Feb. 1776; William Turner, Thos. Moss, Bm.

Ponder, Hezekiah & Martha Leggate, 24 Oct. 1764; Ebenezer
Tomlingson, Bm.; Max. Gallatly, wit.

Pool, John & M. E. Mebane, married 15 Dec. 1857 by E. M.
Forbes, Rector of Christ Church, Elizabeth City.

Portice (?), William & Ann Lewis, 27 Sept. 1785; Henry
Averet, Bm.

Powell, Cader & Nancy Cofield, 23 Dec. 1807; W. M. Peale,
Bm.

Powell, Cader & Celia Williams, 27 June 1827; James L.
Mitchell, George (X) Jenkins, Bm.

Powell, Eldred (X) & Frances Legett, 12 Aug. 1803; Charles
Manning, Bm.

Powell, George (Col.) & Martha Powell (Col.), married 27
Sept. 1868.

Powell, Henry & Polly Bond, 4 Feb. 1802; Henry Lee, Bm.

Powell, Henry & Absala Eason, 7 Feb. 1806; Joseph Eason, Bm.

Powell, James M. & Emergene F. Hancock, 1 Dec. 1865 (lic.).
Married 5 Dec. 1865.

Powell, Jesse & Charity Harrell, 19 Oct. 1798; Lewis Cotten, Bm.

Powell, John & Lavinia Mitchell, married 14 Oct. 1855.

Powell, John R. & Celia F. Powell, married 14 Dec. 1857.

Powell, Miles & Elizabeth Lee, 22 Oct. 1796; Granville (X)
Floyd, Bm.

Powell, W. W. & Mary J. Wynns, married 11 Jan. 1866.

Powell, William & Mary Stallings, 6 Mar. 1800; William
Outlaw, Bm.

Powell, Wm. & Elizabeth Powell, 8 Mar. 1849; William Dalinson (?), Bm.

BERTIE MARRIAGES, 1762-1868

Powell, Wm. & Ann Rebecca Rice, 7 July 1849; Wm. Rice, Bm.

Powell, William L. & Cornelia A. Bishop, 22 May 1857 (lic.).
Married 27 May 1857.

Powell, Willis & Seealey _____, 17 Jan. 1782; William Higs,
Bm.

Powers, Samuel (X) & Sarah Cooper, 3 Nov. 1800; W. Pender,
Bm.

Prevate, Noah (X) & Penney Evins, 6 Sept. 1790; Joseph (X)
Harrell, Bm.

Price, Nezer & Lucinda Jenkins, married 8 Feb. 1855.

Prince, James H. & Pattie Watson, married 15 Oct. 1856
by Leml. S. Reed, Methodist Episcopal Church, South.

Pritchard, Absolum & Sarah Brown, 25 Jan. 1800; Wm. Reed
Sparkman, Bm.

Pritchard, Alsey & Pheby Jernigan, 3 Oct. 1821.

Pritchard, Docton & Lenny M. Green, married 14 June 1857;
John W. Pritchard, Joseph W. Cherry, Drew Pritchard, wit.

Pritchard, Irwin & Lurinda J. Weston, married 21 Nov. 1867.

Pritchard, James & Reany Jernigan, 24 Jan. 1829; George
Farmer, Bm.

Pritchard, Jerry O. & William Ann Gray, married 27 Jan.
1857; James Keeter, Elizabeth Gray, wit.

Pritchard, Jonathan & Patsy Butler, 2 Feb. 1797; John (X)
Butler, Bm.

Pritchard, Lamuel & Nancy Robertson, 18 Feb. 1803; Jonathan
Pritchard, Bm.

Pritchard, Rigdon & Ann Bunch, 29 Feb. 1792; James Pritchard, Bm.

Pritchard, Wm. H. & Milly Jane Bazemore, married 8 Nov.
1860.

Pruden, David & Sarah Sowel, 27 Mar. 1787; Richard Taylor,
Bm.

Pruden, Jacob & Mary Hendrixon, 20 Aug. 1849; Jona. S.
Tayloe, Robt. R. Tayloe, Bm.

Pruden, K. T. & Mary Askew, 6 Sept. 1854 (lic.). Married
7 Sept. 1854.

BERTIE MARRIAGES, 1762-1868

Pruden, Lodowick & Ann Tayloe, 1 Mar. 1799; David Pruden,
Bm.

Pugh, Adam & Antoinette Clark, married 3 Aug. 1866.

Pugh, Francis & Elisabeth Tunstall, 28 Aug. 1792; John
Harlowe, Bm.

Pugh, Francis R. & Mary Ann Rascoe, 5 Dec. 1828; Jona. S.
Tayloe, Bm.

Pugh, George (Col.) & Harriet Miller (Col.), married 21
Dec. 1868.

Pugh, Isaac (X) & Nancy White, 24 Apr. 1830; Wm. R. White,
Bm.

Pugh, John H., Jr. & Elizabeth Gillam, 5 Jan. 1803; Edward M.
Shehan, Bm.

Pugh, Whit (Col.) & Adaline Pugh (Col.), married 28 Sept.
1868; J. J. Jacocks, wit.

Pugh, Whitmel & Bernetta Ruffin, married __ Jan. 1867.

Pugh, Wm. & Victoria Outlaw, married 10 May 1858 by Benj.
S. Bronson, Rector of St. Thomas Church, Windsor.

Pugh, Wm. H. & Frances Hughes, married 28 Aug. 1867.

Pugh, William J. & Elizabeth C. Pugh, married 20 June 1867.

Purdy, Leonard & Ann Clifton, 22 Apr. 1800; John Rowan, Bm.

Purvis, Allen & Anne Gardner, 10 Mar. 1793; Eli Moore, Bm.

Purvis, James H. H. & Mary Ann Davidson, 22 Nov. 1853; Noah
Evans, Bm. Married 22 Nov. 1853.

Raby, Luke & Sally Raby, 26 Aug. 1808; George W. Bond, Bm.

Ramsay, Allen & Sarah Winbourn, 13 May 1833; Wm. H. Green,
Bm.

Rasco, Alexander & Rachel Howell, 30 Apr. 1791; George Folk,
Bm.

Rasco, James & Ann Smithwick, 24 June 1788; John Smithwick,
Bm.

Rasco, William & Rachel Harrell, 13 Dec. 1777; Josiah Harrell, Bm.

Rascoe, Daniel & Polly Hunter, 27 Jan. 1807; Enock Rayner,
Bm.

Rascoe, James & Ann E. Rhodes, 29 Jan. 1828; Samuel South, Bm.

Rascoe, John & Jinnet Skiles, 16 Dec. 1803; Starkey Skiles, Bm.

Rascoe, John & Elizabeth Weston, 8 Apr. 1828.

Rascoe, Thomas & Mildred Sutton, 12 Nov. 1777; Thomas Sutton, Luke Smithwick, Bm.

Rascoe, Washington & Lucinder Hamlin, married 7 Jan. 1867.

Rascoe, William & Mary Twine, married 11 May 1863.

Rasor, Josiah & Elisabeth Sutton, 27 Mar. 1788; Thomas Shehan, Bm.; Thos. Ashburn, wit.

Rawls, Albert & Rena Ann Minton, married 21 Feb. 1860; William C. Dunning, Thos. Minton, Joseph G. Willoughby, James Minton, wit.

Rawls, Jonas & Winney Cook, 20 Aug. 1787; Demsey (X) Cook, Bm.

Rawls, Jonas & Sally Moore, 23 Dec. 1801; William (X) Cook, Bm.

Rawls, Moore & Fannie J. Garrett, married 20 Nov. 1856.

Rawls, Randolph & Margaret Conner, married 19 Nov. 1863.

Ray, Henry (X) & Judith White, 1 Mar. 1794; George (X) White, Bm.

Ray, Henry & Elizabeth Cobb, married 31 Mar. 1868.

Ray, Jacob & Penny Gregory, 6 Jan. 1831; Thomas (X) Ray, Bm.

Ray, James & Polley Nowell, 9 Jan. 1799; Solomon Pender, Bm.

Ray, William (X) & Nancy Todd, 16 Sept. 1793; Samuel (X) Todd, Bm.

Ray, William & Caroline Lecester, married 17 Nov. 1868.

Rayner, Jas. R. & Frances Lawrence, 26 Feb. 1831; Henry D. Johnston, Bm.

Rayner, James R. & Mary Ele Mibane, 2 Apr. 1850; W. P. Gurley, Bm.

Rayner, John & Mary Rayner, married 24 Oct. 1860.

Rayner, Samuel & Harriet Cowand, 25 June 1828; Richd. P. Freeman, Bm.

Rayner, William & Eliza Drew, 20 May 1834; A. Oxley, Bm.

Raynor, James T. & Celia A. Holly, married 12 Dec. 1867.

Redditt, Josiah & Sarah Williams, 14 May 1767; Arthur Williams, John Crickett, Bm.; James Yeates, Isaac Williams, wit.

Redditt, Lodowick & Salley Oxley, 14 May 1795; Hardy Fleetwood, Bm.

Reed, John D. & _____ Ashburn, 20 Dec. 1800; John Harrison, Bm.; W. Hubbell, wit.

Reed, Johnson & Hinney Pugh, 2 Dec. 1823; Jeremiah (X) Simmons, Bm.

Reed, Robert & Mary Pugh, married 30 Dec. 1868.

Reid, George & Francis Boon, married 17 Sept. 1854; Rebecca Hardy, Lucy Boon, wit.

Rhea, Simon D. & Elizabeth Hodges, 7 Apr. 1827; P. M. Conley, Bm.

Rhoads, William & Gilila Jenkins, 22 Aug. 1800; Thomas Sholar, Bm.

Rhodes, Henry & Patience Bridger, 10 July 1772; William Turner, William Bryan, Bm.

Rhodes, Jacob & Winefred Bentley, 21 June 1802; John (X) Bentley, Bm.

Rhodes, Jacob & Fanny Bentley, 11 Dec. 1805; John (X) Bentley, Bm.

Rhodes, James & Salley Smith, 16 Dec. 1794; Jacob Howard, Bm.

Rhodes, James & Anne Outlaw, 23 Oct. 1797; Jonathan Standley, Bm.

Rhodes, James & Sally Burket, 29 Jan. 1849; Joseph (X) Newsom, Bm.

Rhodes, Jesse & Sarah Edwards, 20 Mar. 1799; Malachi Oliver, Bm.

Rhodes, William & Elizabeth Averet, 2 Oct. 1786; Aaron Spivey, Bm.

Rhodes, William G. & Sophia Piland, married 11 Nov. 1862; James B. Steely, Joseph Moore, wit.

Rhods, John & Sarah Carloss (?), 10 Mar. 1780; William Rasco, Bm.

Rice, George W. & Malinda Butler, married 2 Dec. 1861.

Rice, John & Sarah Marcia Early, 7 Sept. 1849; Robt. R. Tayloe, Bm.

Rice, Worley & Martha Hughs, 8 Nov. 1853; H. J. Britt, Bm. Married 8 Nov. 1853.

Rich, Isaac O. & Isaac Rebecca Taylor, married 9 Mar. 1866 (?).

Riddick, James E. & Harriet D. Raby, 14 Apr. 1852; Edward Watson, Bm. Married 22 Apr. 1852.

Riddick, Thos. W. & Sally F. Ward, 25 Sept. 1852.

Ridley, H. B. & Mary E. Speller, 15 Dec. 1849; Jona. S. Tayloe, Bm.

Rigby, Josiah & Prudence Johnston, 2_ July 1808; John Jordan, Bm.

Rigsby, Josiah (X) & Winney Cullifer, 13 May 1796; Charles Barber, Bm.

Rigsby, Wm. & Elizabeth Futrell, 21 Sept. 1863 (lic.). Married 22 Sept. 1863.

Roades, Joshua & Ruth Durry, 18 Jan. 1773; Henry Roades, John Roads, Bm.

Robbins, John & Esther Raby, 27 Apr. 1793; Edward Acree, Bm.

Robbins, Samuel & Sue Sanderlin (Col.), married 25 Dec. 1868.

Roberson, Hardy (X) & Sarah Gains, 12 Jan. 1782; Thomas (X) Hawkins, Bm.; Am__ Gray, wit.

Robertson, Richard & Eliza Thompson, 17 July 1851.

Robinson, John & Mary Castellow, 17 Jan. 1866 (lic.). Married 18 Jan. 1866.

Rodgers, Thos. & Laura Cooper, married 18 Mar. 1866.

Rodgerson, Jos. C. & Jane E. Outlaw, married 5 Dec. 1861; Abram Jenkins, John R. Early, Lewis D. Terry, John L. Outlaw, wit.

Rogers, Ezekiel & Rebecca Parnell, 13 May 1793; Charles Barber, Bm.

Rogerson, Arnold (X) & Macey Rea, 5 Aug. 1839; Jona. S. Tayloe, Bm.; Jno. Freeman, wit.

Rolack, James & Clarisa Allin, married 8 Mar. 1867.

Rooks, Lawrence & Emma Wiggins, married 15 Jan. 1857.

Rose, Peyton R. & Elisabeth Gurley, 16 Jan. 1799; Thomas Church, Bm.

Roulhac, Fayton & Kizzy Watson, 10 Dec. 1866 (lic.). Married 23 Dec. 1866.

Rountree, Abner I. & Mary A. Lambertson, married 23 Dec. 1858.

Rountree, Jackson & Demay E. Lawrence, married 8 Jan. 1862.

Rountree, Obed & Febiby Harrell, 11 Feb. 1771; Jethro Kittrell, Bm.

Rowan, Matthew & Peggy Driver, 6 Feb. 1797; John Rowan, Bm.

Rowe, Micajah & Nancy Rhodes, 15 May 1827; Blake D. Raby, Bm.

Ruffin, Frederick & Elizabeth Cotten, 15 Aug. 1776; Dolphin Drew Young, Bm.

Ruffin, Harrison & Ann Clark, married __ Dec. 1866.

Ruffin, Henry & Treasey Benton, 11 July 1799; James Warren, Bm.

Ruffin, James & Margaret Veal, 22 Dec. 1794; Richard Veal, Bm.

Ruffin, Joseph & Mary Powell, 14 Mar. 1854; Eason Ward, Bm. Married 16 Mar. 1854.

Ruffin, Thomas & Ann Ruffin, married __ Jan. 1867.

Ruffin, William & Martha Bryan, 28 July 1795; William Gray, Bm.

Ruffin, William & Penny Lee, married __ Jan. 1867.

Runnels, Ben & Sarah Stevens, 21 Dec. 1865 (lic.). Married 26 Dec. 1865.

Rutland, James & Elizabeth Rhodes, 4 May 1802; Benjamin Coffield, Bm.

Rutland, James & Sally Bailey, 12 Nov. 1807; Thomas Rhodes, Bm.

Rutland, John & Amelia Nazery, 30 Nov. 1774; Watson (X) Rutland, Bm.

Rutland, Norsworthy & Elizabeth Rutland, 12 May 1828; R. H. Barnes, Bm.

Rutland, Riddick & Jemima Horton, 9 Feb. 1795; Henry Clay Milburn, Bm.

Rutland, Shadrack & Pathena Carter, 5 Nov. 1775; Jesse Cotten, Bm.

Ryan, David & Hannah Garland, 18 July 1833; Marcus C. Ryan, Bm.

Ryan, George & Elizabeth Lockhart, 11 Dec. 1763; Lillington Lockhart, James Lockhart, Bm.

Ryan, Granville & Martha Ann Wiggins, married 28 Apr. 1866.

Ryan, Marcus C. & Margaret E. Legete, 20 Dec. 1827; David Ryan, Bm.

Ryan, Saml. (Col.) & Sarah Fanning (?) (Col.), 24 Mar. 1868 (lic.). Married 26 Mar. 1868.

Saddler, Bennet & Permella Jenkins, 7 Jan. 1852 (lic.). Married 15 Jan. 1852.

Saddler, Bennett & Mary Peele, 3 Jan. 1855 (lic.). Married 9 Jan. 1855.

Sanderlain, Moses (X) & Mourning Demsey, 13 July 1805; Wm. Sanderlain, Bm.

Sanderlain, William (X) & Betsey Demsey, 13 July 1805; Moses (X) Sanderlain, Bm.

Sanderlin, Henry & Margaret Mitchell, married 27 Feb. 1867.

Sanderlin, King (X) & Rachel Brantley, 21 Dec. 1800; Richd. (X) Dempsey, Bm.

Sanderlin, Wm. & Jane Gray, married 5 Feb. 1867.

Sanders, James E. & Eveline E. J. Barrett, married 8 Feb. 1866.

Sanders, James E. & Fannie Holder, married 23 Dec. 1868.

Sanderson, Richard & Sarah Ryan, 19 July 1790; Thomas Ryan, Bm.

BERTIE MARRIAGES, 1762-1868

Sandlin, David & Ferbe Outlaw, married 20 June 1866.

Sasser, John & Polly Driver, 7 May 1775; William Bryan, Kedar Bryan, John McCullens, Bm.

Saunders, John W. & Levona C. Hardy, married 20 Aug. 1854 by Benjamin S. Bronson, Rector of St. Thomas Church, Windsor, at the house of Humphrey Hardy; Humphrey Hardy, wit.

Savage, Isham & Hasty Bishop, married 8 Apr. 1866.

Savage, Oliver P. & Elizabeth F. Jenkins, 21 May 1853; John W. Jenkins, Bm. Married 24 May 1853.

Scott, Joseph & Mary Reed, married 7 Aug. 1856 at the house of Miz Temperance Butler; Thadeus Butler, Emily Butler, Sarah Stewart, wit.

Scull, Joseph J. & Willie A. Ward, married 13 Aug. 1857 by Lemuel S. Reed, Methodist Episcopal Church, South.

Seay, James & Elizabeth Crank, 26 July 1788; Wm. Gray, Bm.

Seay, William & Caroline Murray, 6 Jan. 1803; Micajah Wilks, Bm.

Sessoms, Assad & Nancy Perry, married 25 Apr. 1855.

Sessoms, Coleraine & Penny Ellison, married 27 Sept. 1868.

Sessoms, Hurrell B. & Harriet Eason, 2 July 1827; James Y. _____, Bm.

Sessoms, Nathan & Penelope Perry, 12 Aug. 1806; Andrew Oliver, Bm.

Shahan, Thomas & Rachell Ashburn, 28 Aug. 1766; Thomas Wall, Bm.

Shane, John (X) & Celea Cabell, 5 Apr. 1793; Henry Cullifer, Bm.

Sharp, George (Col.) & Gracy Ryan (Col.), married 24 Dec. 1868.

Sharp, James & Mary E. Powell, 7 Jan. 1863 (lic.). Married 22 Jan. 1863.

Sharp, Thomas H. & Jennie D. Ellyson, 18 Sept. 1866 (lic.). Married 26 Sept. 1866 by Joshua L. Garrett, Elder, Methodist Episcopal Church, South.

Sharrock, Dawson & Hennetta Hardy (Col.), married 9 Feb. 1867; Wm. J. Cherry, Jas. R. Cherry, wit.

BERTIE MARRIAGES, 1762-1868

Sharrock, Thomas & Harriet Lee, married 28 Sept. 1868.

Sharrock, William & Winefred Griffin, 22 Nov. 1792; Josiah Moore, Bm.

Shaw, William & Ann Bird, 15 Jan. 1762; Daniel Worley, Bm.; J. Pearson, wit.

Shawhan, Hady & Elezum (?) Weston, 28 Feb. 1852; William (X) Stone, Bm.; W. N. Mitchell, wit.

Shepherd, John S. & William Ann Moore, 24 Mar. 1853; David Harrell, Bm. Married 24 Mar. 1853; Charles S. Moore, Eliza Waterman, wit.

Sherlock, William & Hetty Winants, 5 Dec. 1805; Wm. Johnson, Bm.

Sholar, Benjamin & Laodicia Thomas, 25 Jan. 1791; Ezekial Thomas, Bm.

Sholar, Cader & Ann Shehan, 22 Apr. 1795; Frederick (X) Shehan, Bm.

Sholar, Joshua (X) & Elizabeth Whitaire, 30 Aug. 1792; John Sholar, Bm.

Sholar, Thomas & Nancy Sholar, 4 Jan. 1790; Benjn. (X) Howard, Bm.

Simmons, James (X) & Elizabeth Doers, 28 Nov. 1786; John (X) Harris, Bm.

Simmons, John & Nancy Dwyer, 10 Sept. 1804; Henry (X) Levain, Bm.

Simmons, Malachi & Jannet Dawson, 10 June 1798; John Duers, Bm.

Simmons, Robert R. & Sarah J. Brooks, 24 Feb. 1863 (lic.). Married 26 Mar. 1863.

Simmons, Wm. J. & Mary D. Burden, married 25 Dec. 1866.

Simons, David L. & Nancy Mizells, married 6 Feb. 1859; Robert Lawrence, John Mizells, wit.

Simons, Henry & Eliza Davis, 26 Sept. 1851; James (X) Bird, Bm. Married 28 Sept. 1851; Benjamin F. King, David C. Simons, wit.

Simons, Joseph & Frances Lee, 23 Nov. 1798; William Robins, Bm.

Simpson, R. D. & Mary E. Gaskin, married 12 Feb. 1856.

Skiles, Charles P. (X) & Mary Capps, 7 Aug. 1824; Wm. (X) Johnston, Bm.

Skiles, Jonathan & Elisabeth Hardy, 10 Nov. 1804; Turner Walston, Bm.

Skiles, Richard & Mary Legett, 25 Feb. 1834; Marcus C. Ryan, Bm.

Skiles, Starkey & Polley West, 12 Aug. 1803; John Miller, Bm.

Skiles, William & Sarah Billops, 15 Jan. 1780; Abishae Turner, Bm.

Skinner, Benjamin & Charity Davis, 20 May 1796; Elisha Higgs, Bm.

Skinner, Edward (Col.) & Mariah _____ (Col.), married 18 Dec. 1868.

Skinner, George F. & Emily Cowand, 27 Oct. 1866 (lic.). Married 28 Oct. 1866.

Skyles, James W. & Nancy Collins, married 13 Sept. 1855.

Skyles, Jonathan T. & Sarah A. Todd, married 18 Mar. 1858.

Skyles, Robert M. & Nancy Todd, married 4 Jan. 1855.

Skyles, Robert M. & Laura F. Collins, married 26 Oct. 1865.

Slade, James P. & Sallie F. Parker, married 4 July 1866.

Slade, John & Nancy T__ King, 28 Oct. 1786; Charles King, Bm.

Slade, John & Jane Baker, 12 Mar. 18__; Alfred D. Winborn, Bm. Married 13 Mar. 1851; H. L. Mitchell, Aaron P. Askew, wit.

Slatter, Solomon & Mary Whitmell, 2 July 1764; James Ryan, Joseph Bryan, Bm.; Humy. Hardy, Thos. Slatter, wit.

Slatter, Thomas & Olive Oxley, 13 Nov. 1777; John Oxley, Bm.; Thos. Hand, William Bryan, wit.

Slaughter, William H. & A. E. Lawrence, married 4 Dec. 1860.

Small, Joseph R. & Martha J. Lawrence, 26 Oct. 1854 (lic.). Married 28 Oct. 1854.

Smallwood, Charles & Harriet J. Clark, 18 Mar. 1850; Wm. B. Smith, Bm.

Smallwood, Daniel F. (Col.) & Emma Smallwood (Col.), married 19 Dec. 1868.

Smallwood, Jesse (Col.) & Edy Smallwood (Col.), 23 Dec. 1867 (lic.). Married 26 Dec. 1867.

Smallwood, Luke & Sylvia Hamlin, married 7 Jan. 1867.

Smallwood, Robert (Col.) & Charlott Ruffin, married 19 Dec. 1868.

Smallwood, Starkey A. (Col.) & Mary W. Ruffin, married 20 Dec. 1868.

Smith, Freeman & Mary Clark, married __ Jan. 1867.

Smith, Henry (X) & Sally Todd, 23 Apr. 1798; William Smith, Bm.

Smith, James W. & Mary Jane Boswell, 15 Jan. 1858 (lic.). Married 21 Jan. 1858.

Smith, Jerry & Elizabeth Thompson, married 11 Aug. 1866.

Smith, John & Sarah Watson, 14 Dec. 1770; William West, Bm.

Smith, John & Elizabeth Vann, 22 Oct. 1777; William Vann, Bm.

Smith, John (X) & Elizabeth Stanton, 29 Jan. 1788; William Bryant, Bm.

Smith, Jonathan (X) & Susanna Miller, 4 July 1798; Reuben Millar, Bm.

Smith, Josiah & Sarah West, 17 Oct. 1767; John Smith, Bm.; William Swain, William West, wit.

Smith, Lewis & Elizabeth Harrell, married 9 Sept. 1855.

Smith, Mills (X) & Rebecca Linton, 15 Feb. 1806; Wm. Powell, Bm.

Smith, Nathan (Col.) & Drucilla Tyler (Col.), 29 Nov. 1867 (lic.). Married 30 Nov. 1867.

Smith, (Dr.) Robert H. & Josephine J. Simons, married 18 Apr. 1855 by Benjn. S. Bronson, Rector of St. Thomas Church, Windsor.

Smith, Stark B. & Joanna Diggs, 5 Feb. 1851; Jos. R. Bird, Bm. Married 5 Feb. 1851.

Smith, Turner (X) & Barsheba Daughtrey, 9 May 1803; Wm. Hodges, Bm.

Smith, William & _____ _____, 19 Jan. 17__; William Wood, Bm.

Smith, William & Rachel Savage, 23 May 1789; Luke Warburton, Bm.

Smith, William (son of Harvy & Lucy Smith) & Jane Lee, married 28 Nov. 1867.

Smith, William A. & Susan Miller, married 4 Oct. 1866.

Smithwick, David & Alice Hyman, married 19 Oct. 1868.

Smithwick, Ebenezer & Sarah Jordan, 4 Feb. 1794; William Sutton, Bm.

Smithwick, Edmondson & Mille Bates, 17 Sept. 1774; James Bate, William Smithwick, Bm.

Smithwick, Humphry & Martha Allen, 24 Feb. 1801; Hardy Boyce, Bm.

Smithwick, John & _____ _____, 30 Dec. 1788; John Sutton, Bm.

Smithwick, John & Susanna Hyman, 2_ Dec. 1804; David Outlaw, Bm.

Smithwick, John T. & Elizabeth A. Pearce, 18 Dec. 1865 (lic.). Married 21 Dec. 1865.

Smithwick, Lanier & Ann Whitfield, 30 Apr. 1800; John Warburton, Bm.

Smithwick, Luke & Elizabeth Watson, 6 Feb. 1773; John Smith, John Davidson, Bm.

Smithwick, William & Mary South, 13 Apr. 1802; John Warburton, Bm.

Smithwick, Wm. H. & Anna J. Webb, married 24 Dec. 1866.

Sorrel, James (X) & Mary Cokran (?), _____; John (X) Kail, Bm.

South, Samuel & Clarisa Hyman, 30 Aug. 1820.

South, William & Sarah Johnston, 20 Dec. 1800; Mills Bonner, Bm.

Sowell, Aquilla & Francis Cullipher, 27 Nov. 1851; Asa (X) Phelps, Bm. Married 27 Nov. 1851.

Sowell, Esekiel (X) & Anne Layton, 22 Dec. 1797; Absolom Pritchard, Bm.

Sowell, James & Peggy Howell, 29 Oct. 1797; Isaiah Smith, Bm.

Spar, William & Margret Briggers, 18 Oct. 1783; John (X) Duglas, Bm.

Sparkman, George (X) & Ruth Holley, 1 Oct. 1786; Edward (X) Turner, Bm.

Sparkman, George (X) & Martha Bryant, 22 Feb. 1791; George (X) Hews, Bm.

Sparkman, James (X) & Francis Hughs, __ Nov. 1790; Hardy Todd, Bm.

Sparkman, Solomon (X) & Sarah Dundelaw, 22 Dec. 1797; James (X) Sparkman, Bm.

Sparkman, Wm. & Elisabeth Hudson, 11 Mar. 1795; Wm. Shaw, Bm.

Sparkman, William & Sarah Surry, 21 Nov. 1800; Wm. R. Sparkman, Bm.

Speller, Cary & Jane Wilson, married 26 Dec. 1866.

Speller, Henry (Col.) (son of Rev. Speller) & Kary Ann Speller (Col.) (dau. of Kary Speller), 21 Oct. 1867 (lic.). Married 3 Nov. 1867.

Spiller, Henry & Sarah Kittrell, 13 May 1800; Lanier Smithwick, Bm.

Spiller, Thomas & Elisabeth Hyman, 24 Apr. 1797; William Luttons, William Smithwick, Bm.

Spivey, Aaron & Elizabeth Grimes, 26 Dec. 1786; William Rhodes, Bm.

Spivey, Aaron & Margt. Pond, 3 Mar. 1832; Thomas Gillam, Bm.

Spivey, James & Charity Fraser, 17 Oct. 1796; Wm. Watford, Bm.

Spivey, Jonathan & Pherby Tart, 15 Feb. 1779; Nathan Tart, Bm.

Spivey, Joshua & Presila More, 13 Oct. 1792; John Moore, Bm.

Spivey, Levin & Margaret Baker, 30 Aug. 1832; Jonathan Standley, Bm.

Spivey, Richard & Pheby Cherry, 3 May 1803; Jas. Tart, Bm.

Spivey, William & Winney Ward, 16 Dec. 1794; Jonathan Spivey, Bm.

Spivey, William & Winefred Ward, 17 Dec. 1794; Jonathan Spivey, Bm.

Spruill, John & Caroline Gurley, married 13 Dec. 1866.

Stall, Jesse (X) & Nancy Parker, 1 May 1829; Luke (X) Parker, Bm.

Stallings, Jimmey (X) & Dicea Jinkins, 7 Oct. 1784; Benjamin (X) Howard, Bm.

Stallings, John & Betsey Jinkins, 30 June 1787; Cader (X) Jinkins, Bm.

Stallings, John & Delitha Duning, 19 Sept. 1789; Samuel (X) Duning, Bm.; James Turner, wit.

Stallings, Josiah & Mary Standley (dau. of Jonathan Standley), 31 Oct. 1766; Jonathan Baker, Bm.; John Johnston, Joseph Wright, wit.

Stallings, Josiah (X) & Winefred Farmer, 15 Dec. 1797; William (X) Donason, Bm.

Stallings, Noah H. & Mary Butler, 17 Nov. 1852; Asa Barnes, Bm. Married 18 Nov. 1852.

Stallings, Phillip & Elisabeth Basemore, 15 Aug. 1798; Josiah Thomas, Bm.

Stallings, Reuben (X) & Mary Morris, 20 Dec. 1784; Joel Cook, Bm.

Stallings, Reuben (X) & Sarah Reasons, 20 July 1804; Nathan (X) Cobb, Bm.

Standley, David (Esqr.) & (Mrs.) Sarah Lassiter, 18 June 1788; Stevens Gray, Bm.; John Slade, wit.

Standley, Jonathan & Polley Watford, 17 Mar. 1799; Ralph Outlaw, Bm.

Standley, Perry & Sarah Whitacher, 20 Sept. 1797; Humphrey (X) Lawrence, Bm.

Standley, William & Penelope Keen, 25 May 1790; William Watson, Bm.

Standley, William & Clarey Baker, 7 Nov. 1796; Larrey Baker, Bm.

Stanton, Robert (X) & Elisabeth Birch, 27 Feb. 1779; William Skiles, Bm.; Wm. McKenzie, wit.

Stark, Williams (of Chowan Co.) & Mary Howell, 7 Dec. 1763; Titus Edwards (of Chowan Co.), Bm.

Starkey, Shimeon (X) & Tabitha Doles, 16 June 1777; John Doles, Bm.

Steel, William & Ann Capehart, 22 Feb. 1794; George P.
Zellner, Bm.

Steel, William & Susannah Fleetwood, 31 May 1797; John (X)
Bird, Bm.

Stevenson, Charles H. & Mary E. Ward, 7 Dec. 1857 (lic.).
Married 9 Dec. 1857.

Stone, Andrew (X) & Salley Heneley, 11 May 1803; David
Gaskins, Bm.

Stone, Edward (X) & Deborah Newborn, 11 Oct. 1785; Thomas
(X) Newborn, Bm.

Stone, Edward & Sarah Brown, 15 Feb. 1793; William Brown,
Bm.

Stone, Jesse (X) & Nancy Brown, 1 Nov. 1796; Sparkman Stone,
Bm.

Stone, William (X) & Sarah Greece (?), 5 Sept. 1800; Henry
(X) Ray, Bm.

Stone, William (X) & Mary Williams, 7 Jan. 1807; B. Hardy,
Bm.

Stuart, James & Luisee Belote, 21 Feb. 1798; Thomas Belote,
Bm.

Stynes, Wm. & Martha White, married 19 Sept. 1867.

Summerlin, John (X) & Josie Maning, 24 Nov. 1777; James
Bentley, William Bradwell (?), Bm.; David Standley, wit.

Sutton, Lewis B. & Sally A. Cooper, married 22 June 1865.

Sutton, Peter & Hasty Rehlache, married 17 Mar. 1866; Martin Harden, Harriett Hoggard, wit.

Sutton, Thomas & Mary Dickinson, 22 May 1787; John Burn, Bm.

Sutton, William & Sarah Warborton, 21 Jan. 1795; Willm.
Burlingham, Bm.

Sutton, (Dr.) Wm. F. & Annie P. Outlaw, married 6 Nov. 1860.

Sutton, William M. & Mary E. Folk, married 22 Feb. 1860.

Swain, Ben H. & Lucy Smallwood, married 16 Feb. 1867.

Swain, Henry (X) & Elisabeth Douers, 23 Mar. 1803; Joseph
Moore, Bm.

Swain, James & Penelope Cary; 20 Dec. 1806; John Dricy (?), Bm.

Swain, Richard (X) & Mary Ward, 6 Nov. 1787; James (X) Ward, Bm.

Swain, Sherad & Mary Lane, 5 Sept. 1792; Richard (X) Swain, Bm.

Swain, Whitmill & Milley Rhodes, 15 Aug. 1806; John Miller, Bm.

Swain, Wm. & Elizabeth White, married 13 Jan. 1855.

Tadlock, Absalom & Sarah Turner, 19 Aug. 1780; William Turner, Bm.

Tadlock, Absalom & Fanny Weston, 6 Dec. 1803; Greenbery Mullen, Bm.

Tadlock, Thomas W. & Susan N. Bayly, married 30 Nov. 1865.

Tadlock, William J. & Annie C. Northcut, married 31 Oct. 1867.

Tarkinton, W. B. & Catharine Griffin, married 2 Apr. 1861.

Tart, James & Pheby Stokes, 10 Jan. 1793; Jonathan Spivey, Bm.

Tart, James & Edith Mitchell, 23 Dec. 1800; D. Eure, Bm.

Tayloe, Abraham, Jr. & Nancy Pike, 8 Aug. 1827; Jesse (X) Farmer, Bm.

Tayloe, David E. & H. E. Outlaw, 2 June 1853; R. J. White, Bm.

Tayloe, Emanual & Josephine Tayloe, 20 Jan. 1866 (lic.). Married 24 Jan. 1866.

Tayloe, James & Sarah Rodes, 12 Sept. 1796; Abraham Harmon, Bm.

Tayloe, Julius & Lucy Butler, 9 Jan. 1866 (lic.). Married 14 Jan. 1866.

Tayloe, Kinchen & Anne Outlaw, 13 Aug. 1795; Thomas (X) Cherry, Bm.

Tayloe, Robert T. & M. F. Williams, married 15 Nov. 1868.

Taylor, Ben & Annis Askew, married 7 Feb. 1867.

Taylor, George & Martha Ann Rice, married 2 Aug. 1856.

Taylor, Reuben & Mary Garre (?), 13 Oct. 1764; Benjamin Barret, Jeremiah Pearce, Bm.

Taylor, Robert R. & Sarah F. Rice, married 21 Feb. 1856.

Taylor, Thomas & Lucy Malone, 22 Dec. 1859 (lic.). Married 29 Dec. 1859.

Temples, Robert & Polley Johnston, 4 Mar. 1803; William Jordan, Bm.

Tennison, Matthew (X) & Milley Hedgpeth, 10 June 1786; Peter (X) Hayse, Bm.

Terry, Lewis D. & Judy C. Outlaw, married 3 June 1858; Wm. G. Marsh, Benja. White, Jos. B. Holloman, wit.

Thomas, Elisha (X) & Polley Burne, 15 Oct. 1805; Henry Bate, Bm.

Thomas, Ezekial & Elisabeth Weston, 2 Mar. 1799; Jonathan Spivey, Bm.

Thomas, G. E. & Dicy Rayner, 30 Oct. 1832; Willie Griffin, Bm.

Thomas, James & Mary Standley, 6 Sept. 1790; Whitmell Whitakar, Bm.

Thomas, John (X) & Sarah Britt, 26 Nov. 1800; Jeremiah Banon, Bm.

Thomas, John & Sally Rayner, 13 May 1829.

Thomas, Jordan (X) & Milley Lassiter, 18 Feb. 1795; James (X) Wilford, Bm.; Wm. N. Green, wit.

Thomas, Joseph & Pernesa Bird, married 4 May 1859.

Thomas, Josiah & Elizabeth Baker, 20 Jan. 1801; William Sowell, Bm.

Thomas, Lewis & Esther Pierce, 29 Jan. 1853; Jonathan White, Bm. Married 30 Jan. 1853.

Thomas, Mike & Betsey Johnston, 4 Aug. 1831; Reddin Bazemore, Bm.

Thomas, William & Milly Jane Cale, married 8 May 1866.

Thomas, Zadock (X) & Dicea Bazemore, 7 Jan. 1793; James (X) Wilford, Bm.

Thompson, Alexander & Elizabeth Mizell, married 21 Feb. 1867.

Thompson, Augustus & Nancy Williams, 24 Jan. 1852; A. H. Thompson, Bm. Married __ ____ 1852.

Thompson, David & Rebecca A. Brown, married 29 Nov. 1866.

Thompson, Doctrin & Deliar Ann Walton, married 11 Aug. 1866.

Thompson, Hampton & Harriet Thompson, 18 Aug. 1866 (lic.). Married 20 Aug. 1866.

Thompson, James (X) & Anne Bazemore, 29 Dec. 1787; Josiah Thomas, Bm.

Thompson, Ketter & Betsey Thompson, married __ Jan. 1867.

Thompson, Lewis F. & Mary A. Swain, married 25 June 1856.

Thompson, Marcus & Matilda M. Barnacastle, married 30 Oct. 1856.

Thompson, Reddick R. & Martha Williams, married 13 Dec. 1855.

Thompson, Turner & Lear Cotton, married 18 Apr. 1866.

Thomson, Charles & Margret Williams, 17 Mar. 1792; David Pruden, Bm.

Thomson, David & Mary Turner, 12 Nov. 1774; James Bates, Thomas Whitmell, Bm.

Thomson, Hezekiah & Mary Pugh, 24 Dec. 1765; Jacob Jernigan, William Junkeson, Bm.; David Standley, wit.

Thornby, James (X) & Penelope White, 23 Sept. 1788; Peleg (X) Belote, Bm.; D. Strachan, wit.

Tillman, William & Polly Granberry, 23 Feb. 1808; James Granbery, Bm.

Todd, Aaron (X) & Winefred Allum, 10 Jan. 1785; Samuel (X) Todd, Bm.

Todd, Aquilla & Sally Hoggard, 3 Jan. 1854; Henry (X) Baker, Bm. Married 21 Jan. 1854.

Todd, Augustus & Harriet Williams, 27 Aug. 1851; Alonzo (X) Britt, Bm. Married 27 Aug. 1851; James Heckstall, Alonzo Britt, wit.

Todd, Elisha (X) & Creecy Lawrence, 25 Oct. 1793; Samuel (X) Todd, Bm.

Todd, Elisha (X) & Senith Smith, 1 Nov. 1797; William (X) Ray, Bm.

Todd, Elisha (X) & Ann Johnston, 24 Dec. 1804; John Mizell, Bm.

Todd, Elisha (X) & Barbara White, 14 Feb. 1839; Bryant (X) White, Bm.

Todd, Elisha & Sally Harrell, 30 Dec. 1865 (lic.). Married 31 Dec. 1865.

Todd, Grandison & Elizabeth Conner, married 3 Jan. 1867; William H. Butler, Thomas J. Harrell, wit.

Todd, Hardy & Sarah Sparkman, 20 July 1793; George (X) Sparkman, Bm.

Todd, Haywood & Malinda White, married 17 May 1865.

Todd, James & Elizabeth Meezles, 11 Oct. 1796; William (X) Todd, Bm.

Todd, James (X) & Mary Mitchell, 19 June 1828; Aquilen (X) Todd, Bm.

Todd, John D. & Sarah F. Cobb, married 2 Feb. 1858.

Todd, John F. & Penelope R. Castellaw, married 25 Jan. 1866.

Todd, Josiah (X) & Nancy Asbell, 10 Dec. 1798; William (X) Todd, Bm.

Todd, Lewis & Martha Corbitt, 16 Apr. 1858 (lic.). Married 25 Apr. 1858.

Todd, Marcus & Elizabeth Harrell, married 8 Oct. 1855.

Todd, Moses & Frnszy (?) Barnes, 10 Sept. 1858 (lic.). Married 12 Sept. 1858.

Todd, Samuel (X) & Winefred Morriss, 28 Nov. 1789; Lamuel (X) Todd, Bm.

Todd, Samuel J. & Mary Morgan, married 19 Dec. 1855; John Butler, William Bird, wit.

Todd, William & Sally Ann Skyles, married 27 Jan. 1867.

Todd, Wm. H. & Tempy White, married 12 May 1862.

Todd, Willis (X) & Ann Curry, 22 Jan. 1831.

Toole, Edward & Mary Holland, 26 Sept. 1764; Jeralden Toole, Bm.

Trotman, Thomas & Winefred Cullens, 3 Mar. 1788; Frederick Cullens, Bm.

Tucker, James (X) & Martha Church, 25 Mar. 1800; Burton Hathaway, Bm.

Turner, James (X) & Mary Mires, 20 June 1796; Elisha (X) Mires, Bm.

Turner, John Blount & Melia Barns, 29 Dec. 1789; James Turner, Bm.

Turner, William & Mary Mullen, 11 Oct. 1780; Absalom Tad-lock, Bm.

Turner, William & Margaret Tayloe, 26 Apr. 1804; Joseph H. Bryan, Bm.

Tyler, Calvan C. & Adaline Williford, 3 Sept. 1833; Aaron O. Askew, Bm.

Tyler, Joseph A. & Martha M. Cox, married 4 Dec. 1866.

Tyler, Napoleon B. & Mary W. Brown, married __ Oct. 1856.

Tyler, Perry & Rachel Hollowell, 8 Feb. 1792; Dempsey Har-rell, Bm.

Tyler, Richard & Jannet Raiby, 15 Oct. 1804; G. Wair, Bm.; Kenneth Clark, wit.

Tynes, John C. & Mary J. Hancock, 9 Nov. 1857 (lic.). Mar-ried 11 Nov. 1857.

Urquhart, Richard A. & Mary R. Norfleet, 5 June 1827; R. A. Urquhart, Abner Andrews, Bm.

Urquahart, Whitmel H. & Frances E. Norfleet, 14 Feb. 1854; Stephen A. Norfleet, Bm. Married 21 Feb. 1854 by Freder-ick FitzGerald, Rector of The Church of the Saviour, at "Woodbourne".

Valentine, David & Winnifred Ann Duns (?), 22 Nov. 1850 (?); Kader Biggs, Bm.

Valentine, David A. & Mary J. Miller, 12 Aug. 1863 (lic.). Married 13 Aug. 1863.

Van, Edward (X) & Salley Higs, 7 Feb. 1788; John (X) Harrell, Bm.

Van Pelt, James & Catharine Hugh, 10 Jan. 1793; George (X) Hughs, Bm.

Vass, John (X) & Frances Gordfree, 15 Dec. 1787; Notting-ham Monk, Bm.

Veale, Richard & Anne Harrell, 6 Apr. 1800; Arnold Milburn, Bm.

Veale, William & Agness Veale, 17 Nov. 1798; Thomas Veale, Bm

BERTIE MARRIAGES, 1762-1868

Virgin, William & Anne King, 15 Aug. 1763; Henry Gibbons, Bm.

Wair, George & Ann King, 15 Sept. 1804; Francis Pugh, Bm.

Wair, Willis & Melbre Cross, 18 Aug. 1798; Thomas Sholar, Bm.

Walker, Milton & Ella Walton 21 Dec. 1865 (lic.). Married 28 Dec. 1865.

Walker, N. H. & Permelia Kemp, 21 Dec. 1853; Leo. Clary, Bm. Married 22 Dec. 1853; Geo. W. McGlauhon, Zd. S. Simmons, wit.

Waller, Bryan & Martha Tadlock, 27 May 1834.

Walton, Lewis & Jane Clark, married 28 July 1866.

Walton, Ryan & Annis Hardy, married _____.

Warburton, James & Winefred Smith, 22 Jan. 1772; James Sweatman, Bm.

Warburton, John & Clarissce Knott, 2 Sept. 1800; William Sutton, Bm.

Ward, Aquilla & Mary E. Williams, 16 Mar. 1857 (lic.). Married 17 Mar. 1857.

Ward, Frank & Delitha Hassell, married 28 Aug. 1862.

Ward, Frank W. & Mary A. Davis, married 20 Sept. 1857.

Ward, George (X) & Ann Oxley, 6 Nov. 1804; John Oxley, Bm.

Ward, Hillory & Elizabeth Cowand, 15 May 1850; Wm. M. D. Wynns, Bm.

Ward, James (X) & Sarah Swain, 21 Nov. 1795; Hugh Hardy, Bm.

Ward, James & Zilpha Todd, married 5 Nov. 1856.

Ward, James & Sallie Coffield, married 7 June 1860.

Ward, James & Ann D. Henry, married 24 Jan. 1867.

Ward, Jordan, & Hanah Ward, 6 Dec. 1798; Richard (X) Swain, Bm.

Ward, Joshua & Seloey (?) Ward, 19 May 1797; William P. Hardy, Bm.

Ward, Nathaniel & Linna Mariah Daughtery, married 30 Mar. 1855; William Stone, wit.

101

BERTIE MARRIAGES, 1762-1868

Ward, Shelton & Happy Castellow, married 21 Apr. 1859.

Ward, Timothy & Martha Watson, 11 Oct. 1787; Stephen Outterbridge, Bm.

Ward, Whitmill & Sarah A. Lawrence, 25 Aug. 1853; F. W. Ward, Bm. Married 25 Aug. 1853.

Ward, William & Marina Conger, married 3 Oct. 1856.

Ward, William & Sarah F. Hughes, married 3 Nov. 1865; David Thompson, Wm. Cowan, wit.

Ware, Gerrad & Charlotte Keen, 27 Aug. 1787; Samuel Harrell, Bm.

Warren, James & Mary Cherry, 21 June 1788; William Gray, Bm.

Wartry, William & Martha A. Frame, 20 Mar. 1828; Gray B. King, Bm.

Wateridge, William & Mildred Thompson, 31 Mar. 1821; William Deanz, Bm.

Waterfield, Wm. Alfred & Margaret White, 5 Sept. 1863 (lic.). Married 6 Sept. 1863.

Waterman, John & Eliza Rawls, 6 July 1831; John Stewart, Bm.

Watford, John (X) & Rachel Cowand, 16 Apr. 1791 (?); George Cowand, Bm.

Watford, (Dr.) W. B. & A. P. Askew, 4 Nov. 1861 (lic.). Married 7 Nov. 1861.

Watford, William (X) & Priscilla Frazer, 18 May 1779; Harday Watford, Bm.

Watford, William, Jnr. & Elisabeth Watford, 12 Dec. 1801; Josiah Asbell, Bm.

Watson, Edward & Elizabeth Ann Lee, married 21 Aug. 1856 by Leml S. Reed, Methodist Episcopal Church, South.

Watson, James & Lilla Bishop, married 30 Mar. 1866.

Watson, John & Sarah Collins, 25 June 1764; James Bentley, Bm.

Watson, Rhoden & Eveline Tayloe, married 29 Nov. 1868.

Watson, William & Mary Benbury, 14 Nov. 1777; John Watson, Thomas Watson, Bm.; Thos. Harrison, wit.

Watson, William & Sarah R. Speller, married 7 Apr. 1860.

Watts, Lewis & Rachel Jernagan, 25 Apr. 1785; Mark Morgan, Bm.

Weaver, John Binam (X) & Mary Handley, 26 Mar. 1788; George Crutch, Bm.

Webb, Frank & Clara Ward, married 2 Aug. 1866.

Webb, Jona. R. & Martha Magruder, 11 Oct. 1832; M. C. Ryan, Bm.

Webb, Lawrence Smith & Keziah Wood, 23 Jan. 1794; Thomas Harden, Bm.

Webb, Thomas & Mary Nicholls, 3 Dec. 1767; Humphrey Nicholls, Robert Butterton, Bm.

Webb, Memer (?) B. & Sally F. Nicholls, 5 July 1827; Jno. B. Williams, Bm.

Wells, Henry & Mary Bates, 17 Nov. 1772; Henry Bates, Bm.

Wesson, A. J. & Nicie Dempsey, married 25 Nov. 1868.

West, Josiah & Elisabeth Legett, 23 Aug. 1799; Joseph Carley, Bm.

West, Robert & Susannah Lockhart, 7 Nov. 1792; John Burn, Bm.

West, Thomas & Catherine Legett, 5 June 1802; John Knott, Bm.

West, Thomas & Salley Bate, 30 Nov. 1803; Absalom Tadlock, Bm.

West, William & Mary Bate, 15 Aug. 1806; John Miller, Bm.

Weston, Amoss (X) & Winefred Mitchel, 23 Sept. 1780; Joseph (X) Mitchel, Bm.

Weston, Edward (of Northampton Co.) & Fanny White, married 3 June 1855; Jeremiah H. Bunch, Asa Cooper, Anderson Casper, wit.

Weston, Ephraim & Mary Jordan, 22 Feb. 1791; Thomas Weston, Bm.

Weston, Ephraim & Catherine Barnes, 22 Mar. 1797; John Weston, Bm.

Weston, Ephraim & Harriet Heyman, 16 July 1828; Thos. L. Weston, Bm.

Weston, Josephus & Martha Futrell, 20 Jan. 1853; Miles (X) Hewett, Bm. Married 20 Jan. 1853.

Weston, Malachi & Surenda Burdan, married 20 Dec. 1860.

Weston, R. A. & Thomas M. Worley, 13 Nov. 1850.

Weston, Thomas S. & Martha Gregory, 7 July 1827; E. B. Weston, Bm.

Weston, William & Susanna Hoggard, 1 Jan. 1822; Zacheris Cherry (?), Bm.

Whitacre, Whitmell & Easter Sholar, 26 Apr. 1790; Cader Sholar, Bm.

Whitaker, John E. & Mary Ross, 13 Dec. 1854 (lic.). Married 18 Dec. 1854; Thos. H. Speller, Lewis T. Bond, wit.

Whitaker, Solomon & Rachel Boon, married 21 Feb. 1866.

White, Alfred J. & Martha Floyed, married 14 Mar. 1867.

White, Amos (X) & Susanna Harrell, 7 Jan. 1804; George (X) Ward, Bm.

White, Augustus & Martha Ann Mizells, married 16 Feb. 1862.

White, Benjamin & Nancy C. Todd, married 14 Jan. 1864.

White, Bryan & Eliza Todd, married 23 Dec. 1863.

White, Cader (X) & Polley White, 28 Nov. 1798; John (X) White, Bm.

White, David (X) & Judeth Carols (?), 20 Feb. 1803; Jacob (X) White, Bm.

White, David & Jestenna Smith, married 18 June 1856.

White, David & Frances Perry, married 23 June 1859.

White, Ephraim (X) & Sarah Hardy, 30 Oct. 1780; Ezekiel (X) White, Bm.

White, Ezekiel (X) & Mary Harrison, 30 Oct. 1780; Ephraim (X) White, Bm.

White, Frederick (X) & Judith Byrum, 15 June 1792; Noah (X) White, Bm.

White, Frederick & Francis Collins, 26 Nov. 1853; John (X) Davis, Bm. Married 27 Dec. 1853; James Heckstall, William Stone, wit.

White, George (X) & Leeda White, 23 May 1794; Reuben (X) White, Bm.

BERTIE MARRIAGES, 1762-1868

White, George & Patsey Powell, 7 Apr. 1827; Meedy White, Bm.

White, George & Elizabeth Gaskins, 14 May 1834; Benjamin Gaskins, Bm.

White, Henry, Senr. & Martha A. J. Freeman, married 10 Mar. 1856.

White, Hezekiah & Susan Ann Bowen, 6 Jan. 1855 (lic.). Married 11 Jan. 1855.

White, Jacob (X) & Elisabeth Hoggard, 4 July 1804; William (X) White, Bm.

White, James K. & Mary Freeman, married 17 May 1855.

White, James R. & Mary Ann Baker, married 1 Jan. 1857.

White, Jesse & Sophia Lary, 12 Feb. 1785; Jethro (X) Butler, Bm.

White, John & Penelope Dorsey, 27 Mar. 1771; James Yeats, Caleb Hooten, Bm.

White, John & Frances Hoggard, 18 May 1831; Jno. Williams, Bm.

White, John & Mary Britt, 14 Aug. 1854 (lic.). Married 15 Aug. 1854.

White, John & Elisabeth Jane Baker, married 7 May 1858.

White, Joseph & Caraline Mitchell, 10 Mar. 1854; C. Johnson Cowand, Bm. Married 21 Mar. 1854.

White, Joseph & Martha Butler, 27 Feb. 1864 (lic.). Married 28 Feb. 1864.

White, Joseph J. & Martha White, 22 Dec. 1852; Holloway E. (X) Bowen, Bm. Married 23 Dec. 1852.

White, Joshua & Mary Early, 25 Feb. 1851; John Rice, Jr., Bm. Married 27 Feb. 1851.

White, Josiah & Eliza Cowand, 11 Sept. 1851; Joseph White, Bm. Married 11 Sept. 1851.

White, King & Martha Britt, 22 Jan. 1788; John Pierce, Bm.

White, Martin & Martha Harrison, 30 May 1808; Jesse (X) White, Bm.

White, Meedy (X) & Salley Tiner, 22 Aug. 1801; Jethro (X) Butler, Bm.

White, Noah (X) & Talitha Collins, 15 June 1792; Fredk.
White, Bm.

White, Noah A. & Sally Pearce, married 18 Jan. 1860.

White, Noah A. & Penny Jernigan, married 7 Mar. 1867.

White, R. C. & Nanny Quinnby, married 25 Oct. 1865.

White, Reuben (X) & Abigail Cale, 9 Sept. 1794; George (X)
White, Bm.

White, Reuben & Nancy Jane Mizells, 20 Dec. 1865 (lic.).
Married 21 Dec. 1865.

White, Solomon & Patsey Outlaw, 19 Dec. 1800; John Cowand,
Bm.

White, Solomon & Kiddy Cowand, 10 Apr. 1832; William Cowand,
Bm.

White, Stephen (X) & Patience Britt, 13 Feb. 1795; Jethro
(X) Butler, Bm.

White, Van Buren & Priscilla Mizells, married 11 Apr. 1860.

White, Walton & Mary Butler, married 1 Aug. 1855.

White, Watson L. & Penelope Lassiter, married 20 Nov. 1866.

White, William & _____ Keen (widow), 28 Feb. 1784; John
Johnston, Bm.

White, William (X) & Elizabeth Arquart, 30 Dec. 1797; John
Hicks, Bm.

White, William & Mary Mizells, 15 Nov. 1854 (lic.). Married
16 Nov. 1854.

White, William & Sarah Henry, 4 Mar. 186_ (lic.). Married
6 Mar. 1862.

White, William H. & Sally Mizell, married 15 Jan. 1858.

White, William N. & Emma Eliza Evans, married 4 Apr. 1867.

White, William T. & Sabrina Conner, married 8 Jan. 1856.

White, William W. (Col.) & Amanda Jane Tayloe (Col.), 11
Nov. 1867 (lic.). Married 14 Nov. 1867.

Whitfield, Benja & Elizabeth Acres, 13 Feb. 1777; John Watson, Bm.

Whitmell, Thomas & Penelopy Pugh, 20 Oct. 1768; Thomas Hunter, Bm.

Wiggins, James (X) & Prudence Runnels, 24 Dec. 1828; Lewis (X) Boon, Bm.

Wiggins, John (of Halifax Co.) & Elizabeth Bevins (widow), 30 Sept. 1766; Samuel Johnston, Bm.; John Gregorie, wit.

Wiggins, Joseph & Dorcas Flood, 5 Oct. 1853 (lic.). Married 7 Oct. 1853.

Wiggins, Mathias (X) & Pressy Tabert (Mulatto), 3 Jan. 1786; James (X) Page, Bm.

Wiggins, William & Margretta Ann Bell, married 7 Aug. 1858; Henry Bird, Tabithy Overton, wit.

Wilder, Absolom & Ann Britt, 8 July 1779; George Kittrell, Bm.

Wilder, Adkin (X) & Celia Hoggard, 18 Apr. 1808; Jesse (X) Wood, Bm.; Baldy Ashburn, wit.

Wilder, Jackson & Elizabeth Ward, 23 Dec. 1852; Stark B. Smith, Bm. Married 23 Dec. 1852; Britton Jones, wit.

Wilder, Thos. R. & M. E. Ricks, 27 Dec. 1865 (lic.). Married 28 Dec. 1865.

Wilford, Alanson & Martha Butler, married 5 Apr. 1855.

Wilford, Archibald (X) & _____ Broadwell, 1 Nov. 1786; James (X) Wilford, Bm.

Wilford, Henry & Sarah Phelps, 27 Feb. 1852; Henry Wilford, Bm.; W. N. Mitchell, wit. Married 28 Feb. 1852.

Wilford, Isom (X) & Clary Thompson, 13 Aug. 1796.

Wilford, Isom & Winefred Thomas, 7 Sept. 1801; John (X) Brayboy, Bm.

Wilford, James (X) & Judeth Thomas, 16 Jan. 1786; David Collins, Bm.

Wilford, James & Jarsey Capehart, 19 July 1827; Levy (X) Castellaw, Bm.

Wilford, Lewis (X) & Cloe Holley, 10 Nov. 1781; William Bryan, Edward (X) Wilson, Bm.

Wilkins, William & May Garrett, 14 Dec. 1802; Jacob Garrett, Bm.

Wilkins, Wm. H. & Temperance Tyner, married 5 Nov. 1856.

Wilkison, Frederick (X) & Milley Drury, 15 Mar. 1780; William Griffin, Bm.

Wilks, James & Elizabeth Harrell, 6 Mar. 1779; Joel Harrell, Bm.; Jas. Wm. Bryan, wit.

Wilks, James (X) & Mary Thorowgood, 20 Apr. 1779; Henry
Rhodes, Bm.

Wilks, Micajah (X) & Anice Leay, 27 Sept. 1791; James Wilks,
Bm.

Willaby, Isaac (X) & Elizabeth Willaby, 22 Aug. 1792; William (X) Willaby, Bm.

Willey, Matthias & Mary Walston, 6 Oct. 1795; John Cooper,
Bm.

Williams, Albert & Lisina Williams, married 20 Aug. 1866.

Williams, Asa F. & Ann Powell, married 17 Aug. 1865.

Williams, Benjamin & Elizabeth Harrell, 28 Jan. 1850;
Aquilla (X) Ward, Bm.

Williams, Charles & Olive Whitacre, 26 Apr. 1774; Whitmell
Hill, Bm.

Williams, Cornelius & Polly Eborn, 22 Sept. 1866 (lic.).
Married 24 Sept. 1866.

Williams, Daniel (Col.) & Eliza Rountree (Col.), 1 Jan.
1868 (lic.). Married 4 Jan. 1868; Juley Ann Lee, Charity
Armistand, Andrew Baldin, Befume Menay, wit.

Williams, Doctrin & Eliza Hoggard, married 26 July 1866;
Charles Meezells, Jeremiah Harrell, wit.

Williams, Elisha & Sarah Jasey (?), 24 Mar. 1775; John
Johnston, Bm.

Williams, Elisha (X) & Harriet Ward, 19 Feb. 1834; William
(X) Williams, Bm.

Williams, Elisha & Penelope Morriss, 9 Sept. 1864 (lic.).
Married 15 Sept. 1864; William D. Mitchell, Aaron O.
Askew, wit.

Williams, Ezekiel & Sarah Farrar, 14 Feb. 1791; David (X)
Curry, Bm.

Williams, George & Elizabeth Ward, 14 Oct. 1839; Ben (X)
Williams, Bm.

Williams, Henry & Frances Stall, married 8 Feb. 1859.

Williams, Henry & Fannie Pugh, married __ Dec. 1866.

Williams, Henry Fletcher & Laura Slade Pugh, 12 June 1846.

Williams, Henry G. & Lucy Tunstall, 14 Aug. 1793; Francis
Pugh, John Harlowe, Bm.

Williams, Henry H. & Pelelope J. Turner, 10 Feb. 1851;
Joseph B. Lee, Bm.

Williams, Isaac & Nancy Bunch, 7 Dec. 1769; Jeremiah Bunch,
Henry Bunch, Jr., Bm.; Thos. Turner, Jr., wit.

Williams, Jack & Louisa Smallwood, married __ Jan. 1867.

Williams, James & Susanna Baker, 6 Nov. 1799; Daniel Young,
Bm.

Williams, James & Nancy Henry, 27 Dec. 1826.

Williams, James & Mary Holloman, married 9 Dec. 1859.

Williams, James L. & Susan Mizells, married 17 Mar. 1856.

Williams, James M. & Susan A. Cobb, married 5 Feb. 1868.

Williams, John & Rachel Thompson, married 10 Jan. 1855.

Williams, John & Mary E. Langdale, married 28 Dec. 1855.

Williams, John & Catharine Pugh, married 21 Dec. 1859.

Williams, John F. & Margaret White, 27 Dec. 1854 (lic.).
Married 18 Jan. 1855.

Williams, Jos. T. & Frances R. Bird, married 1 Oct. 1868.

Williams, Leroy & Sally Hyman, 12 May 1828; Aquilla Hyman,
Bm.

Williams, Lewis & Sally Nowell, married 18 Jan. 1866.

Williams, Morgan & Sally Edwards, 8 Sept. 1778; Browning
Williams, Bm.; Abram B. _____, Chas. C._____, wit.

Williams, Sam & Dilla Williams, married __ Jan. 1867.

Williams, Sandy (Col.) & Delia Capehart (Col.), married
22 Dec. 1868.

Williams, Thomas & Martha Nixon, married 28 Feb. 1867.

Williams, William (X) & Sarah Lawrence, 18 Aug. 1795;
Richard (X) Barnicastle, Bm.

Williams, William (X) & Mary Eliza White, 11 Oct. 1832;
Levi (X) Hughs, Bm.

BERTIE MARRIAGES, 1762-1868

Williams, William & Jane Askew, 15 Mar. 1852; William D.
Askew, Bm.

Williams, William & Catharine White, married 18 Jan. 1860.

Williams, William R. & Mary E. Green, married 8 Dec. 1861.

Williams, Zadock (X) & Juda Kale, 22 Dec. 1783; John (X)
Sawell, Bm.

Williamson, Oliver & Sarah Ruark, 20 July 1798; John (X)
Moore, Bm.

Williford, A. J. & Mary R. Matthies, married 16 Jan. 1862.

Williford, James J. & Lurinda V. Dunning, married 16 Dec.
1868.

Williford, John & Polly Freeman, 19 Jan. 1804; Josiah
Jenkens, Bm.

Williford, John Joseph B. (X) & Elizabeth Farmer, 18 Oct.
1851; William (X) Harris, Bm. Married 28 Oct. 1851.

Williford, John V. & Martha A. Williford, married 9 Apr.
1861.

Williford, R. H. & Julyann Matthies, married 16 Jan. 1862.

Williford, Stephen & Lucinda Pruden, 20 Aug. 1849; Jona.
S. Tayloe, Robt. R. Taylor, Bm.

Williford, William & Jennet Early, 7 July 1827; John (X)
Laster, Bm.

Willoughby, Joseph & Mary Wallace, 13 June 1850 (lic.).
Married 20 June 1850.

Wilson, Isaac (X) & Sally White, 9 Sept. 1808; Noah (X)
White, Bm.

Wilson, James (X) & Silyey Outlaw, 24 Aug. 1803; Jacob (X)
Outlaw, Bm.

Wilson, John & Elizabeth White, married __ June 1855.

Wilson, Turner & Roxanne West, 9 Dec. 1850; Wm. H. Rhodes,
Bm.

Wilson, William (X) & Elizabeth Cooper, 7 July 1787; William Skiles, Bm.

Wilson, William Turner & Malinda A. Halsey, 27 Oct. 1866
(lic.). Married 28 Oct. 1866.

BERTIE MARRIAGES, 1762-1868

Wimberly, Abram & Ann Spive, 28 Mar. 1765; Moses Spivey, Bm.

Wimberly, William & Elisabeth Harrell, 9 Jan. 1783; Frederick Wimberly, Bm.

Winborn, Alfred D. & Levena Marsh, 13 Nov. 1852; I. P. Freeman, Bm. Married 13 Nov. 1852.

Winborn, James & Jane Lawrence, married 3 Nov. 1865; John A. Rhodes, Ryan Butlar, wit.

Winborn, William & Jane Parker, married 5 Dec. 1859.

Winburn, Benjamin (X) & Sarah Jones, 26 May 1804; Fredk. James, Bm.

Wingate, William & Nancy Cook, 4 Apr. 1804; Henry Fleetwood, Bm.

Wixen, James & Harriet E. Hines, 13 Mar. 1848; W. G. Worley, Jona. S. Tayloe, Bm.

Womble, Edwin & Martha Hancock, 24 Oct. 1857 (lic.). Married 25 Oct. 1857.

Womble, Joseph H. & Clara E. Copeland, 13 Nov. 1865 (lic.). Married 23 Nov. 1865.

Wood, Cullen & Sally Freeman, 12 Aug. 1791; Joshua Freeman, Luke Warborton, Bm.

Wood, Jesse & Elenor Martin, 3 Mar. 1794; William Smith, Bm.

Worth, George & Mary A. Watson, 9 Sept. 1852; Jas. H. Cherry, Bm.

Wright, David & Mary Armistead, 24 June 1795; Jordan Armistead, Bm.

Wyatt, Esau & Tempey Johnston, 7 Feb. 1804; David (X) Curry, Bm.

Wynn, William D. & Frances E. Wilford, married 17 Apr. 1860.

Wynns, George & Milley Watford, 21 Oct. 1807; Wm. Watford, Jr., Bm.

Wynns, George A. & Mary J. Burdan, married 24 May 1860; Alfred D. Winborn, Wm. McD. Wynns, Jos. W. Sessoms, William H. Slaughter, wit.

Wynns, Watkin W. & Mary Williford, 14 May 1821; G. Wynns, Bm.

Wynns, Wm. McD. (son of Wright Wynns) & Martha F. Powell
(dau. of Richard & Mary Powell), married 12 Nov. 1868.

Yates, William E. & Mary A. Bayly, married 26 Dec. 1855.

Yeates, Edward & Elizabeth Lealch (?), 23 Dec. 1826; Samuel
South, Bm.

Yeates, William & Ava Waters, 13 June 1827; Samuel South,
Bm.

Yeats, Edward & Mary Weston, 21 Sept. 1795; Solomon Weston,
William Sutton, Bm.; Joseph Fletcher, wit.

Yeats, James & Avarilla Walston, 4 Feb. 1767; Josiah Redditt, Bm.

Yeats, James & Mary Griffin, 2_ Dec. 1804; Miles Bonner,
Bm.; Jos. Blount, Griffen Yeats, wit.

Yeats, Solomon (X) & Elizabeth Davis, 1 Jan. 1834.

Yeats, Thomas & Rachel Shehan, 25 Feb. 1793; William Griffin, Bm.

Yeats, William & Charlotte Whitledge, 7 July 1787; William
Griffin, Bm.; Thos. Ryan Butler, wit.

Young, Dolphin Drew & Absola Bell, 15 Aug. 1776; Frederick
Ruffin, Bm.

Young, John & Martha Averet, 4 Feb. 1785; Willis Powell, Bm.

Young, Thos. M. & Matilda Durdan, 20 Feb. 1854; Joshua (X)
Harrell, Bm. Married 21 Feb. 1854.

Zollner, George Peter & Mary Capehart, 17 Mar. 1789; George
Capehart, Bm.

Bazemore (cont.)
Eliza 26
Fanny 24
Hannah E. 12
Henry 6
James 31
Jesse 42
Jesse, Jr. 7
Mary E. 7
Milly Jane 81
Nancy 49
Penelope 10
Penny 73
Reddin 97
Stephen 17
Thomas 78
Bazmore, Abisha 7
Beasly, Thos. 46
Belch, Priscilla 13
Bell, Absola 112
Frederick 8
Margretta Ann 107
Belote, Catharine 19
Fanny 74
Henry 12
John 19
Luisee 95
Nancy 30
Noah 7, 50, 64
Peleg 98
Silas 41, 56
Tabitha Cumi (?) 61
Thomas 95
Benbury, Mary 102
Benson, Elizabeth 63
William 33
Wm. 58
Benthall, Levy 38
Bentley, Elisabeth 7
Elizabeth 5
Fanny 84
Frances 64
James 95, 102
John 29, 37, 84
Mary 5
Patsey 18
Winefred 84
Benton, Elisabeth 58
Milley 58
Treasey 86
Bevins, Elizabeth 107
Biggs, Kader 100
Rebecca 56
Billops, Sarah 90
Billups, Ransom 10
Richard 64
William West 2
Birch, Elisabeth 94
Bird, Ann 89
Edy 57
Elizabeth 7, 55
Frances R. 109
Henry 107
Jacob 35
James 16, 89
John 41, 95
Jos. R. 91
Martha 14
Mary Catharine 43
Pernesa 97
Rutha Ann 55
Susannah 74
W. E. 39
William 9, 99
William C. 11
Wm. W. 34, 36
Bishop, Cornelia A. 81
Hasty 88

Bishop (cont.)
Lilla 102
Louisa Camilla 41
Nancy 9
Permelia 50
Venus 9
Wm. 27
Bittle, Andrew 7, 9
John 52
Blackson, Henry 3
Blake, James 43
Blanchard, Martha 42
W. 62
Blount, Ams. 24
Chloe 21
Edmund 62
John L. 10
Jos. 112
Permelia 36
Volley 12
Wyrriott 10
Boldin (Baldin ?), Andrew 80
Bond, George W. 82
Jno. W. 30, 63, 64
John 76
Lewis T. 104
Margaret 63
Margaret M. 64
Mary 54
Mary E. 12, 43
Patty 10
Penelope 50
Polly 80
Rhodea 10
Sally 10
Sarah W. 10
Thomas 36, 50
Bonner, Miles 5, 10, 20, 26, 56, 112
Mills 92
Sarah 8
Boon, Francis 84
Lewis 107
Lucy 84
Mary 10, 47
Rachel 104
Booth (?), Temperance 56
Bosman, Elizabeth 45
Boswell, Betsey 16
Charles 41
Elisabeth 61
Margaret 9
Mary 9, 67
Mary Jane 91
Rachel 39
Ritta 78
Tempy 49
Thomas 19
Thos. 10
Winefred 41
Boulton, Elisabeth 50
Bowden, Georgianna 72
Bowen, Ann 49
Anna 31
Benjamin 11
Celia 16
Cornelius 11, 22
Darcas 23
Hardy 26
Henneritta 33
Holloway E. 105
Huldah 23
Jesse 11, 22
Joshua 11, 23
Margaret Winnifred 11
Polly 4
Rebecca 28

Bowen (cont.)
Sarah 57
Susan Ann 105
William E. 16
Bowens, Sarah Frances 52
Bowers, Prudence 22
Bowin, Nathan 5
Bowls, Jonas 71
Boyce, Demsey 46
Elizabeth 9
Hardy 92
John 11
Penelope 25
Boysson, Ellenor 14
Bradwell (?), William 95
Brannet, (?) 44
James 44
Brantley, Martha 65
Rachel 87
Brassell, Patience 25
Brayboy, John 107
Lydia 6
Susan 55
Brewer, Eliza 26
Brickell, Lavinia 56
Bridger, Joseph J. 48
Patience 84
Powell 62
Robert 49
Robert, Jr. 65
Robert M. 15
Briggers, Margret 93
Brimage, Mary 64
Brinkley, Elisha 67
Britain, Nancy 68
Briton, James 50
Britt, Alonzo 98
Ann 107
Betsey 60
Eliza 48
H. J. 78, 85
Loving 71
Martha 6, 105
Mary 105
Mary Ann 42
Patience 106
Sarah 97
Britton, J. F. 64
J. L. 7
Virginia A. 73
Broadwell, (?) 107
Brogden, Aaron 24
Betsey 24
Mary 24
John 12
Luckey 17
Nelly 48
Sarah 12
Thomas 12, 13
William 13, 72
Bronson, Benj. S. 10, 47, 82
Benjamin S. 52, 88
Benjn. S. 2, 36, 40, 91
Brooks, Sarah J. 89
Brown, Angelica 24
Arthur 7
Caroline 16
David 79
Feribe 69
Martha 17, 78
Mary 1, 48
Mary E. 8
Mary W. 100
Morin 50
Nancy 38, 95
Penelope 4
Rebecca A. 98

116

Brown (cont.)
  Robert 9
  Rowan 48
  Sarah 81, 95
  Sarah Jane 65
  Sylvia Ann 64
  William 95
Browne, Mary 18
Bruce, Elisabeth 32
  Jeremiah 32
Bryan, Elisabeth 75
  Francis 60
  Jas. Wm. 108
  Jesse 30, 75
  Jos. H. 39
  Joseph 52, 90
  Joseph H. 100
  Kedar 88
  Lewis 43
  Martha 86
  Morning 76
  William 14, 84, 88, 90, 107
  Wm. 36, 49
Bryant, Jeaney 46
  Martha 93
  Martha A. C. 54
  Susan 26
  William 91
Buck, Stephen 41
Bunch, Amanda E. 49
  Ann 79, 81
  Celia 31
  Cullen 48
  E. J. 15
  Embrey 14
  Frederick 15
  Harriette 64
  Henry 109
  Jer. H. 48
  Jeramiah, Jr. 21
  Jeremiah 15, 109
  Jeremiah H. 49, 103
  Mary 15
  Micajah 15, 49
  Nancy 109
  Nehemiah 42
  Winafred 70
  Winefred 49
Burdan, Bittie 42
  Elizabeth 21
  James 67
  Julia (Mrs.) 27
  Mary J. 111
  Phoebe E. 67
  Priscilla 67
  Surenda 104
Burden, Ann E. 2
  Balinda 67
  James 19
  Mary D. 89
  Mary J. 66
  Mary 1. 32
  Milly 33
  Phoebee 60
  Sally Ann 53
Burges, Margaret 62
Burke, Thomas 31
Burket, Ann 44
  Mary 57
  Milissa Ann 9
  Sally 84
Burlingham, Willm. 13, 95
  Wm. 24
Burn, James 52
  John 95, 103
Burne, Polley 97
Burras, Salley 55

Burress, Mary 42
Bustin, Clairacy 76
Butes (?) (Butler ?),
  Thos. Ryan 75
Butlar, Ryan 111
Butler, (?) 15
  Ann Rebecca 68
  Cene 72
  Clarissa 9
  Curbey 20
  Curre 18
  Edith 6
  Elizabeth 23, 31
  Emiline 9
  Emily 88
  Eunice 78
  Jethro 105, 106
  John 9, 81, 99
  John L. 65
  Kenneth 20, 42
  Lucy 96
  Malinda 85
  Marcus 20
  Martha 105, 107
  Mary 6, 94, 106
  Mary Temperance 23
  Patsy 81
  Peggy 67
  Ryan 9, 62
  Sally F. 45
  Sarah 78
  Temperance 55, 88
  Thaddeous H. 9
  Thadeus 88
  Thos. Ryan 64, 112
  William H. 99
  Wm. H. 16, 45
  Worley 18
Butterton, Mary W. 11
  Robert 103
  Robt. 50
  Sarah 18
Bynum, Polly 7
Byram, Eva 54
  Mary 76
  Priscilla 20
  Sally 5
  Sarah A. M. 67
  Starkey 20
Byrd, John 47
Byrum, Ann 18
  Elizabeth 25
  Judith 104
Cabell, Celea 88
Cale, Abigail 106
  Charney 17
  Clarissa 12
  Elizabeth 14
  Jersey 22
  Martha 4
  Mary (Mrs.) 18
  Milly Jane 97
Calloway, Sarah 30
  Thomas 61
Callum, Willis 49
Campbell, Jas. 62
Canada, Jennet 17
Canaday, David 17
Canady, Sarah 44
Cannady, Frances 59
  Penelope 70
Capehart, Ann 95
  C. 20
  Cullen 18
  Delia 109
  Elisabeth 63
  Emily 54
  George 112

Capehart (cont.)
  James 37
  Jarsey 107
  John 22
  Keddy 40
  Margaret 18
  Mary 112
  Mary M. 18
  Nancy 41
  Nancy E. 54
  Pauline A. 18
  Phyllis 21
  Sarah 34
  Sarah E. 18
  Sophia E. 63
  William 59
Capehearte, Gefson 80
Capps, Mary 90
  Milly Ann 28
Caps, Moses 28
Car, Jonathan 47
Carley, Joseph 103
Carloss (?), Sarah 85
Carney, Absalom 33
  Ann 33
  Thomas 88
Carols (?), Judeth 104
Carr, Lucy 13
Carter, Annie H. 10
  Mary 18
  Mary Ann 72
  Nancy 23, 33
  Pathena 87
Cary, Penelope 95
Casper, Anderson 5, 19, 53, 103
  Calvin 49
  Caroline 26
  Elizabeth 45
  Fanny 62
  George 19
  Margaret 5
  Mary 38
  Mary J. 26
  Thomas 49
Castalaw, Prudence 5
Castallow, Cary 49
Castellaw, Asa 19
  John W. 74
  Levy 107
  Penelope 57
  Penelope R. 99
  Thomas 15
Castello, Caroline 8
Castellow, Caroline 78
  Christian 79
  Elizabeth 20, 35
  Happy 102
  Harriet 25
  Isaiah 20
  James 20
  Mary 85
  Sarah 54
Castelow, Harriet 23
Champion, Sarah 27
Chapel, Heziah 7
  Rachel 26
  Wm. T. 6
Cherry, Aaron 21
  Celia E. 6
  James H. 69
  Jas. H. 111
  Jas. R. 88
  Jn. B. 68
  Joseph W. 81
  Joshua 17
  Martha 4
  Mary 102

117

Cherry (cont.)
  Mary E. 15
  Perlina 66
  Pheby 93
  Rosa A. 21
  Sally Ann 74
  Sarah 31
  Soln. 13
  Solo., Jr. 68
  Solomon 52
  Thomas 6, 74, 96
  Will. 24
  William W. 65
  Wm. 21
  Wm. J. 21, 42, 88
  Wm. W. 34, 66
Cherry (?), Zacheris 104
Cherrye, Bethiah 52
Cheshire, Jos. Blount 41,
  46
Church, Ann 30
  Martha 99
  Thomas 62, 86
  Thos. 21
Churchwell, Henry 1
  Polly 4
Clark, Ann 86
  Antoinette 82
  Harriet J. 90
  Jane 101
  Kenneth 6, 27, 41, 42,
    100
  Margaret E. 22
  Marinna 13
  Mary 91
  Mary Catharine 57
Clarkson, Saml. R. 45
Clary, Leo. 101
  Virginia S. 57
Claxton (?), E. 28
Clayton, Deborough 70
  Margaret 57
Clifton, Ann 6, 82
  Anny 5
  Elizabeth 20
  James 72
  Levin 20
  Martha 72
  Peter 74
Cob, Sarah 30
Cobb, Charles 70
  Chloe 37
  Christian 64
  Crissey 79
  Dolley 62
  Elisabeth 26, 60
  Elizabeth 14, 19, 83
  Frances 50
  Happy 30
  Henry 4, 7, 18
  Joanna 28
  Margaret 11
  Mourning 7
  Nancy 18
  Nathan 66, 94
  Patsey 18
  Penelope 11
  Rutha 9
  Sally E. 78
  Sarah 29
  Sarah F. 99
  Susan A. 109
  Thomas 22
  Thomas H. 20
  William 2
  Winney 48
Cockran, Marth 61
Coffield, Benjamin 70, 86

Coffield (cont.)
  Delila 35
  Isaac 23
  Martha A. R. 72
  Martha S. 4
  Mary 23
  Sallie 101
  Sarah E. 29
  William 4, 23
Cofield, Elisabeth 37
  Nancy 80
Coggin, William 58
Cokran (?), Mary 92
Cole, Grace 49
  John W. 52
  Martha 62
  Mary 15
  Polly 9
  Sally 20
Collins, Angy Elizabeth
  62
  David 107
  Dudith 31
  Francis 104
  James 52
  Laura F. 90
  Luke 59
  Nancy 90
  Sarah 102
  Talitha 106
  Tempy 47
  Thomas 46
  William 69
Combes, David 19
Conger, Marina 102
  Sally 51
Conley, P. M. 84
  Wm. 58
Conner, Elizabeth 99
  Margaret 83
  Marina E. 25
  Noah 20
  Rebecca 25
  Sabrina 106
  Sarah 43
  Susanda 44
  Winnifred 32
  Wright 25
Cook, Benja. 66
  Benjamin 50, 60
  Demsey 83
  Elisabeth 5
  Elisha 13
  Ellen 37
  James 25
  Joel 36, 94
  John 25
  Martha C. 40
  Nancy 111
  Rubbin 25
  Sarah 12, 77
  Tabitha 25
  William 5, 83
  Winney 83
Cooper, Alice 62
  Asa 103
  Augustus 60
  Elizabeth 110
  Frances 23
  Hester 68
  Jesse 10
  John 30, 108
  Joseph 62
  Laura 85
  Mariah 26
  Mary E. 49
  Milley 17
  Sally 75

Cooper (cont.)
  Sally A. 95
  Sarah 81
  Sarah H. 52
  William 5
Copeland, Clara E. 111
  Elizabeth 36
  John 6
  Will 47, 75
  Wm. J. 6
Copland, Freeman 26
Corbert, Elisha 11
  John 26, 49, 59
Corbet, Amanda S. 27
  Elisha 29
Corbitt, Martha 99
Cotten, Cullen 29
  Elizabeth 86
  Godwin 76
  Jemima 33
  Jesse 87
  Lewis 1, 80
Cotton, Godwin (Mrs.) 52
  Lear 98
  Margaret 52
  Mary C. 36
  Peggy 55
Cowan, Ann 21
  Wm. 102
Cowand, C. Johnson 105
  Eliza 105
  Elizabeth 101
  Emily 90
  George 102
  Harriet 84
  Hetty 36
  John 106
  Johnson 16
  Kiddy 106
  Mady 31
  Margaret 51
  Rachel 102
  William 27, 106
Cox, Ezekiel S. 27
  Francis 56
  Georgeanna 5
  Henrietta 12
  Margaret 56
  Martha Jane 14
  Martha M. 100
  R. H. 14, 77
  W. J. 77
Craddoc, Rebecca 73
Crank, Elizabeth 88
Crickett, John 38, 84
Cross, Melbre 101
  Patience 44
Crutch, George 103
Crutchdow, Anna F. 61
Cuff, Nancy 21
Cullen, Barbara 77
Cullens, Frederick 99
  Sarah 36
  Winefred 99
Cullerpher, Easter 56
Cullifer, Chloe 28
  Harriet 30
  Henry 88
  Martha 64
  Nancy 28
  Winney 85
Cullipher, Agnes 41
  Angelina 55
  Casanda 78
  Creecy 57
  Elizabeth 23, 57
  Francis 29, 92
  Harriet 79

Cullipher (cont.)
  Henry 28
  Leeda 45
  Miles 29
  Nathaniel 56
  Penny 48
  Ritta 75
Curl, Charney 8
Curry, Affa 70
  Ann 99
  Banajah 29
  Bernajah 29
  David 29, 108, 111
  Elizabeth 4
  Jacob 60
  James 29
  Wilie 27
  Willie 29
Dale, Elizabeth 42
  Emily 16
Dalinson (?), William 80
Daren, John 63
Daughtery, Linna Mariah 101
  Nancy 30
Daughtrey, Barsheba 91
Davidson, Elisabeth 59
  John 23, 92
  Martha Catharine 78
  Mary 33
  Mary Ann 82
  Mary E. 16
Davis, Annis 43
  Celea 38
  Charity 90
  Delila 40
  Eliza 89
  Elizabeth 29, 60, 112
  George 30
  James 19
  John 104
  Mary A. 101
  Nancy 45
  Smith 30
  William 30
Davison, Mary 76
  Nancy 76
Dawson, George 18
  Hannah 10
  Jannet 89
  John 44
  Mary 14
  Penelope 62
  Richard 64
Deanes, William 30
Deanz, William 102
Dempsey, Anne 57
  Eliza 24
  Elizabeth 17
  James 60
  Nicie 103
  Opaliza 63
  Richd. 87
  Wealthy 31
  Whitmell 31
  William 57
Demsey, Betsey 87
  Elisha 31
  Mourning 87
  Richard 31
Denty, Francis 3
Dickinson, Mary 95
Diggs, Joanna 91
Dodrill, James 31
  John 3, 75
Doers, Elizabeth 89
Doles, John 94
  Tabitha 94

Donaldson, Jane 60
  Temperance Ann 67
Donason, William 94
Donnison, Margaret 19
Dorsey, Penelope 105
Douers, Elisabeth 95
Douglas, John 4
Dowers, Margaret 24
Downs, Emaline 40
  Jesse 40
  Mary 40
  Milton 78
  Willie 40
Drew, Eliza 84
  Joseph W. 48
  Mary 35
Drew (?), Mary E. 34
Dricy (?), John 95
Driver, Peggy 86
  Polly 88
Drizzle, John 24
Drury, Janey 53
  Milley 107
Duers, John 89
Dugin, Elisabeth 10
Duglas, John 93
Duke, Abraham 27
Dundalow, Polly 16
Dundelaw, Sarah 93
Dundston (?), Lucy 29
Dunes (?), Winny 41
Duning, Charles 3
  Delitha 94
  Elisabeth 56
  Mary 3
  Minney 49
  Samuel 31, 94
Dunning, A. J. (Mrs.) 40
  Andrew J. 19, 32, 78
  Anne 42
  Annelizer 31
  Celey 24
  Celia F. 15
  Lethena 32
  Lurinda V. 110
  Martha Ann 25
  Mary 33
  Sallie M. 32
  Sarah 54
  William 34
  William C. 83
  Wm. C. 53
Duns (?), Winnifred Ann 100
Dunsmore, Axum 14
Dunstan, Edmund 29
Durdan, Matilda 112
Durry, Ruth 85
Dwyer, Elenor 63
  Nancy 89
Earley, Anne 31
  Betsy 50
  Lidia 25
  Sarah 25, 73
Early, Asa 71
  Asa F. 19
  Jane E. 37
  Jennet 110
  John 4
  John R. 85
  Mary 105
  Mason C. 32
  Parthena 60
  Penece 13
  Sarah Marcia 85
  Wm. J. 53
Eason, Absala 80
  Celia 3

Eason (cont.)
  Harriet 88
  Joseph 80
  Mary 21
  Penelope 36
  Rachel 37
Eborn, Polly 108
Edwards, Eliza. 7
  John 33
  Polly 74
  Sally 109
  Sarah 84
  Titus 64, 94
Elliot, Sally Ann 39
Ellis, Sarah 20
Ellison, Penny 88
Ellissun, Zach. 12
Ellyson, Jennie D. 88
Eperson, Elisabeth 26
Etheridge, Mary 21
Eure, D. 96
Evans, Charles H. 33, 48
  Emma Eliza 106
  Eveline 73
  John 44
  Jonas 62
  Julia 38
  Maria 19
  Mary 44
  Noah 82
  Peter 4
  Sarah 44
  Susan 47
  Wright 30
Evins, Penney 81
Fannin, Thos. 68
Fanning (?), Sarah 87
  T. E. 26
  Thomas E. 13
Farless, Mary Ann 1
Farmer, Christian 2
  Elisabeth 67
  Elizabeth 110
  George 81
  James 42
  Jesse 96
  Judy 42
  Martha 31
  Rachel 40
  Winefred 94
Farrar, Sarah 108
Farror, Rachel 64
Fergason, W. A. 16
Ferguson, W. A. 14
Fig, Christopher 18
FitzGerald, Frederick 100
Fleetwood, Elizabeth 8
  Hardy 34, 84
  Henry 111
  John 16, 34
  Sarah 34
  Susannah 95
Fletcher, Joseph 112
Flood, Christian 40
  Dorcas 46, 107
  Mary Jane 4
Floyd, Bellison 25
  Elisabeth 25
  Granville 80
  Priscilla 12
  Rachel 74
  Samuel 49
Floyed, Martha 104
Flury, Henry 64
Folk, George 82
  Mary E. 95
  Polly 77
  William 9

Folks, Benjamin 59
Forbes, E. M. 80
Ford, Nancy 49
Forest, Elizabeth 69
Forman, Benjamin 62
Frame, Martha A. 102
　Penelope 29
Frances, Sterling 77
Francis, Margaret Ann 43
Fraser, Charity 93
Frazer, Priscilla 102
Frazier, Alexr. 70
Freeman, Aaron 35, 75
　Celia 18
　Elizabeth 20, 36
　Hardy 52
　Harriet 67
　I. P. 111
　Jno. 86
　John 31, 68, 69
　Joshua 22, 111
　Martha A. J. 105
　Mary 105
　Nancy 71
　Polly 110
　Rachel 35
　Richd. P. 84
　Sally 111
　Sarah 71
　Winny 36
Futrell, Elizabeth 85
　Martha 103
　Nancy 2
Gains, Sarah 85
Gale, Cornelius 22
Gallatly, Max. 80
Gardner, Anne 82
　Elizabeth 44
　James A. 36
　Jason 10, 42
　John 53
　John J. 7
　Lurany 6
　Martin 36
　Mary Ann 44
　Patience 53
　Sarah 30
Garland, Hannah 87
Garre (?), Mary 96
Garrett, Ann 79
　Fannie J. 83
　Jacob 37, 73, 107
　Jesse 37
　Joshua L. 88
　Louisa E. 22
　Martha E. 27
　May 107
　Nancy 58
　Raches 24
　Sallie J. 17
　Winefred 60
Garriss, W. D. 37
Gary (?), John 30
Gaskin, Ann 64
　Mary E. 89
Gaskins, Adaline J. 46
　Anne 63
　Ann R. 14
　Augustus 46
　Benjamin 105
　Betsey 41
　David 95
　Elizabeth 60, 105
　George 37
　Nancy 68
　Polly 44
　Salley 8
Gatling, Jos. 20

Gelmon, Elizabeth 50
Gibbons, Henry 101
Gilbert, Esther 8
Gill, Ann Eliza 3
　Lavonia 61
　Martha E. 36
　Mary W. 3
Gillam, B. 26
　C. Rebecca 28
　Elizabeth 82
　Mary Virginia 33
　Moses 3
　Thomas 93
　Winafred E. 8
Gilliam, Frances 66
　H. A. 68
Gilman, Mary 77
Glauhan, Martha 28
Glesson, Elizabeth 27
Glessone, Martha 25
Godwin, Marina 53
Godwine, Elizabeth 9
Goff, Caela 43
Gordfree, Frances 100
Granberry, Polly 98
Granbery, James 98
　Langley 70
　Wm. 38
Grant, Elizabeth 51
　Eliza Jane 16
　Sarah M. 30
Gray, Am__(?) 85
　Amelia 22
　Elizabeth 69, 81
　Frances 41
　George 76
　Jane 87
　Jonas 77
　Lydia 50
　Stevens 10, 18, 52, 58,
　　94
　William 19, 60, 86, 88,
　　102
　William Ann 81
　William Lee 69
　Wm. 10, 15, 58
　Wm. Lee 10
Greece (?), Sarah 95
Green, Elizabeth 55
　G. N. 38
　Harriet 24
　Lenny M. 81
　Mary E. 110
　Sarah 71
　W. H. 31
　William H. 56
　Wm. H. 9, 74, 82
　Wm. N. 97
Gregorie, John 107
　Margt. 11
　Martha 104
　Penny 83
Griffen, Nancy 5
　William 3
Griffin, Catharine 96
　Martin 70
　Mary 112
　Micajah 28
　Patty 6
　Thomas 5
　William 39, 77, 107,
　　112
　Willie 16, 97
　Willis 57
　Winefred 89
Grigory, Margaret 57
　Mary Jane 79
　Thomas 20

Grimes, Elizabeth 93
Groves, (?) 34
Grymes, Saml. 58
Gurley, Caroline 94
　Elisabeth 86
　W. P. 83
Hadom, George Jernigan 39
　Samuel Jernigan 40
Hagathay, Sarah 50
Hale, Joshua 40
　Lodowick 53
Hall, Ellen 76
　Frances 61
　Sarah 76
Hallom, Sally 63
Halsey, Malinda A. 110
　Mary 74
Hambleton, Nanny 77
　William 77
Hamlin, Lucinder 83
　Sylvia 91
Hancock, Emergene 80
　Martha 111
　Martha W. 12
　Mary J. 100
Hand, Thos. 90
Handley, Mary 103
Hardee, Charles 40
Harden, Levi 5
　Martin 95
　Thomas 12, 25, 103
Hardey, Elizabeth 9
　Martha 52
Hardin, Polly 79
　William D. 79
Hardison, Jasper 8
Hardy, Anne 8
　Annis 101
　B. 95
　Charles 20, 37
　Edw. A. 76
　Edward 52
　Edy 7
　Elisabeth 90
　Harriet 55
　Hennetta 88
　Hugh 101
　Humphrey 88
　Humy. 90
　James 8, 15
　John 18, 34
　Jonathan 18
　Lemuel 41
　Levona C. 88
　Rebecca 84
　Sally 37
　Sarah 41, 104
　William 41
　William P. 101
　Wm. Edward 47
　Wm. Parrot 50
Hare, Mary 67
Harison, George 42
　Reuben 35
Harlow, John 26
Harlowe, John 82, 109
Harman, Jonathan 4
　Maria 21
　Nicholas 42
　Winny 71
Harmon, Abraham 96
　Anne 34
　Charles 21
　Charles W. 42
　Eli 42
　Elizabeth 17, 21
　Martha 42
　Richard T. 21

120

Harmon (cont.)
Sarah 32
Harrel, Pricilla 2
Harrell, Amos 42
Ann 20
Anna 34
Anne 100
Barbara 50
Benjamin 42
Catherine 66, 71
Celia 56
Charity 80
David 44, 89
Dempsey 100
Dicey 56
Elisabeth 53, 111
Elizabeth 4, 31, 91,
99, 108
Febiby 86
Frances 42
George D. 23
James 44
Jeremiah 108
Jesse, Jr. 71
Joel 44, 53, 108
John 14, 100
John C. 55
Joseph 77, 81
Joshua 64, 112
Josiah 33, 63, 82
Josiah, Sr. 44
Judith 40
Mary 21
Mary N. 77
Mason 32
May Ann 32
Rachel 82
Raney 64
Renney 77
Rhody 76
Sally 99
Samuel 102
Sarah 36, 44
Sarah E. 25
Susanna 104
Tempy 13
Thomas 42
Thomas J. 45, 99
William 22
Zilpha 42
Harreson, Ruben 63
Harrill, Mary 65
Harris, Amos 61
John 89
Mary A. 5
William 110
Harrison, Elizabeth 54
John 84
John W. 56
Martha 105
Mary 104
Reuben 48, 68
Ritta 69
Thomas 69
Thos. 102
Harrisson, Reuben 16
Hassel, Luvina 13
Hassell, Delitha 101
Mary Ann (Mrs.) 48
Hast, Sary 35
Haste, Samuel 8
Hathaway, Burton 99
Hattian, Ruben 25
Hawkins, Ann 61
L. E. 60
Mary 31
Rachel 60
Susan Ann 55

Hawkins (cont.)
Thamer 28
Thomas 85
Hayes, Anne 45
Elisabeth 73
James 46
Hays, Hannah 46
Hardy 45
Harriet 66
Sarah 37
Hayse, Judah 46
Penelope 35
Peter 97
Sarah 75
Heckstall, Acenith 7
Deborah 73
Hannah 18
James 46, 98, 104
Theodore 46
Hedgpeth, Milley 97
Hendrixen, William 70
Hendrixon, Mary 81
Hendry, Robert 24
Heneley, Salley 95
Henry, Ann D. 101
Arabella 70
Celia A. 22
John 60
Maria 10
Nancy 35, 109
Robert 61
Sarah 106
Herrington, James 34
Hewett, Miles 103
Hews, George 93
Heyman, Harriet 103
Hicks, John 53, 60, 106
Higgins, David 2
Higgs, Betty 46
Elisha 90
Elizabeth 1
Jacob 77
Moore 27
Sarah 49
Whitmell 25
William 13, 38
Higs, Salley 100
William 81
Hill, Elizabeth 52
Henry 5, 52
John 46
Milly 13
Nancy 62
Whitmell 108
Willie J. (Mrs.) 40
Wm. 46
Hilliard, Francis W. 63
Hines, Elizabeth J. 39
Harriet E. 111
Hinson, Ellenor 29
Hinton, Micajah 38
Hobbs, Ann M. 42
Harriet 46
Joseph 47
Lavina 44
Martha Ann 35
Silas 44
Hobdy (?), Repsey 44
Hodder, Elizabeth 73
Sarah 33
Sarah Ann 60
Hodge, Patience 75
Hodges, Elizabeth 84
Ellen E. 54
Fannie G. 37
Jesse 22
John 72
Mary 37, 79

Hodges (cont.)
William 37, 79
Wm. 91
Hogard, Susanna 13
William 47
Hoggar, Mary 34
Hoggard, Anny 11
Betsey 22
Celia 107
David 32
Elisabeth 105
Eliza 108
Elizabeth 49, 54
Frances 105
Frasieur 47
George 16
Harriet 55
Harriett 95
Jesse 66
John 48, 62
Kiddy 20
Marthena E. 39
Mary 54
Mary Ann 45
Nancy 41
Patrick 48
Penelope 20
Sally 98
Sally A. 19
Seth 48
Susanna 104
Wm. 48, 69
Hogwood, Calvin 18, 41
Holden, Elisha 58
Holder, Abram 45
Aggy 66
Augustus 9
Edy 15
Elisha 11, 14
Fannie 87
Henrietta 13
Levina 14
Mariah 3
Mary A. 45
Sally 20
Susanah 11
Holladay, Hannah 24
Holland, Mary 99
Rachel 75
Saly 75
Sewell 75
Holley, Cloe 107
Elisabeth 63, 66
Emiline 69
John 20
Josiah 50
M. 72
Mary 33, 77
Prudence 10
Ruth 93
Thomas 33
Holliday, Asia 56
Elizabeth 56
Susan 10
Holloman, George 17
Jos. B. 78, 97
Mary 109
Nancy 19
Sally Ann 18
William 67
Hollomon, Jersey 53
Hollon, Frederick 31
Hollowell, Rachel 100
William 50
Holly, Celia A. 84
Elisabeth 19
Patsy 37
Hooks, Alexander 37

Hooks (cont.)
Ann 30
Hooten, Caleb 105
Hopkins, John 25
Sarah 25
Hoppkins, Winnefred 25
Horn, Emily J. 61
Mary 9
Horne, Joseph 43
Horne (?), Lawrence 64
Horne, Moses 50
Horton, Anne 36
Jemima 87
House, Edey 10
Geo. 70
Martha 58
How, Alexr. 41
Elizth. 41
Howard, Benjamin 50, 94
Benjn. 89
Celia 73
Jacob 84
Mary M. 75
Reddick 73
Sally 14
Howe, Sarah 15
Howell, Ann 63
Mary 94
Peggy 92
Rachel 82
Sam 70
Hubbard, Ann 77
Mary 16
Hubbell, W. 84
Hubbord, Elizabeth 77
Mary 11
Hudson, Elisabeth 93
Huff, Cornelius 19, 53
Hugh, Catharine 100
Hughes, Allen (?) 51
Charlett 68
Frances 82
George 68
James 51
Judah 16
Sally 72
Sarah F. 102
Thomas 27
Hughs, David 51
Francis 93
George 100
James 51
Levi 109
Martha 27, 85
Mary 26, 78
Mary E. 31
Nancy 20
Pernecia 23
Reuben 77
Hunt, Mary 38
Hunter, John 72
Polly 82
Robert 63
Senith 35
Synthey 52
Thomas 22, 106
William 35
Huson, Sally 61
Hyman, Aquilla 109
Alice 92
Clarisa 92
Elisabeth 93
Hugh 5
Lemuel 62
Mary 29
Sally 109
Samuel G. 36
Sarah 9

Hyman (cont.)
Susanna 92
William 8, 62
Irvin (?), John 62
Irvings (?), Mary 44
Irwin (?), John 16
Ives, Mary 1
Jackson, Phereby 15
Jacobs, Margt. A. 68
Peggy 4
Jacocks, Ann 73
J. J. 68, 82
Jona. 28
Jonathan 73
James, Andrew 53
Benjamin 53
Elisabeth 36
Fred R. 53
Fredk. 111
Fredrick 53
Jeremiah 53
Keziah 53
Mariah 24
Mary 53
Jarnagan, Needham 74
Jasey (?), Sarah 108
Jenkens, Abram 32
Elitha 19
Josiah 110
Jenkins, A. 19
Abraham 32
Abram 40, 67, 85
Cader 53
Charles T. 4, 78
Elizabeath 29
Elizabeth F. 88
George 65, 80
Gilila 84
John W. 32, 40, 88
Joseph 20, 78
Lodwick 32, 45
Lucinda 81
Lucy 53
Martha 29
Mary 45
Permella 87
Sally 33
Winborn 53
Jernagan, Rachel 103
Jernegan, Lewis 4
Jernigan, Anne 54
Arthur 54
Benja. 54
Benjamin 54
Elizabeth J. 69
Ethelred 54
Jacob 98
James 17
Louay 9
Martha 15
Mary 48
Nancy 54
Nancy O. 26
Nathaniel 54
Penelope 71
Penny 106
Pennyritta 48
Pheby 81
Polly 4
Reany 81
Sarah 3, 54
Jernikin, Godwin 40
Jinkens, Lod 32
Jinkins, Betsey 94
Cader 94
Dicea 94
Elisabeth 50
Lewis 50

Jinkins (cont.)
Mary 67
Temperance 63
Job, Samuel 76
Jobe (?), Fereby 4
Johnson, Belenda 45
Elizabeth 57
James 22
Littleton 31
Sally E. 19
Wm. 89
Johnston, Ann 98
Betsey 97
Celia 15
Henry D. 83
John 14, 22, 55, 57, 58,
62, 77, 94, 106, 108
Joseph 59
Nancy 27
Patsey 75
Penelope 6
Polley 97
Prudence 85
Saml. W. 11
Samuel 107
Sarah 92
Tempey 111
William 38
William W. 6, 58
Wm. 90
Joiner, Deborah 55
Joliff, Emily "Emma" 53
Leora C. 66
Jones, Ada 14
Alfred 12
Benja. 66
Britton 107
David 56
James 24
Joel 43
Levina A. 2
Mary 31
Matilda 5
Nancy 40
Polly 63
Rebecca 62, 71
Sally 66
Sarah 13, 111
Thomas 61
Jordan, Francis 38
Hannah 39
J. P., Jr. 62
James 75
James B. 28, 35
John 85
Joseph 62
Marcia 30
Margaret 62
Martha 57
Mary 57, 103
Mary Elizer 72
Prudence 59, 62
Sarah 2, 92
William 70, 97
Junkeson, William 98
Kail, John 92
Kale, Elizabeth 64
Juda 110
Keane, Polly 77
Richd. 77
Keen, (?) 106
Charlotte 102
James 9, 71
Milley 17
Moses 57, 63, 71
Penelope 94
Sarah 24
Keeter, Asenith R. 28

Meezels/Mizell, Starkey E. 23
 Thomas 23
 William 23
Meezles/Mizell, Elizabeth 99
Meezlle/Mizell, Mornin 29
Meizells/Mizell, Sally 47
Mellon, Reuben 65
Melone, Drury 11, 17
Menay, Befume 108
Mesells/Mizell, Winefred 29
Mezall/Mizell, James 54
Mezel/Mizell, Sol 55
Mezells/Mizell, Aaron S. 48
Mezill/Mizell, Charles 16
Mibane, Mary Ele 83
Michel, Winny 23
Miers, Ann Mariah Augustus 70
 Nathan, Jr. 35
 Patsey 48
Milburn, Alexander 66
 Arnold 100
 Elizabeth 10
 Henry Clay 87
 Samuel 45
Millan, Reuban 68
Millar, Reuben 91
 Soloman 67
Miller, Ann 31
 Ann J. 66
 Benj. 8
 Caroline 19
 Emily 9
 Harriet 82
 I. W. 1
 John 90, 96, 103
 Josiah 1
 Lewis 65, 68
 Martha A. 55, 69
 Martha E. 35
 Martha J. 35
 Mary 71
 Mary J. 100
 Nancy A. 65
 Nathaniel 28
 Nelly 29
 Nelly Ann 4
 Patricia 1
 Rebecca 47
 Reuben 46, 65
 Salamer 65
 Sally 73
 Solomon 14
 Susan 92
 Susanna 91
 W. C. 48
 Will C. 9
 William C. 62
 Winnefred 68
Mills, Charles 53
Milton, Dickison 65
Minton, James 83
 Lavinia 25
 M. J. 25
 Margaret 42
 Polly 79
 Rena Ann 83
 Thos. 83
Mires, Benjn. 46
 Elisha 100
 Elizabeth 48
 Mary 39, 100
 Nathan 72
 Winefred 40

Misel/Mizell, Samuel 22
Misell/Mizell, Clary 65
Misells/Mizell, Sarah 65
Mitchel, Elisabeth 70
 Happy 74
 John 72
 Joseph 15, 20, 103
 Mary 68
 Penelopey 20
 Phebe 15
 Rhodea 72
 Sarah 20
 Susanna 11
 William 69
 Winefred 27, 103
 Zekial 66
Mitchell, Ann 42
 Betsey 32
 Cader 34
 Caraline 105
 Celia 74
 Edith 96
 Francis 14
 Franklin V. 20
 Gaven H. 66
 Geo. 68
 H. L. (Dr.) 32, 90
 Harriet 15
 Henry L. 32
 James 40
 James L. 80
 Jane 21
 Jas. L. 53
 John 3, 21, 25
 Josiah 67
 Lavinia 80
 Margaret 87
 Martha 67
 Martha E. 67
 Mary 99
 Mary E. 53, 63
 Milley 75
 Nancy 40
 Perry 67
 Rhoda 61
 Sarah 18
 Thomas 3
 Thos. 64
 W. D. 19
 W. M. 23
 W. N. 57, 89, 107
 W. P. 47
 William 16, 67
 William D. 59, 108
 William N. 65
 Wm. D. 66
 Wm. N. 73
 Wm. Z. 20, 53
 Wright 67
 Zadock 11, 34
Mizel, Sol. 69
 Starkey E. 22
Mizell, Aaron 68
 Absaley 59
 Ann Elizabeth 55
 Elizabeth 43, 97
 Emiline 48
 Frances 39
 John 47, 68, 71, 98
 Joseph 72
 Kiddy 17
 Lucinda J. 73
 Maria Frances 43
 May C. 51
 Moses S. 48
 Penny 48
 Sally 106
 Sarah 23

Mizell (cont.)
 Starkey 23
 Timothy 67, 68
Mizells, Ailsey 19
 Amelia 6
 Betty 37
 Eli 79
 Jane 65
 John 69, 89
 Judith 29
 Martha Ann 104
 Martha C. 49
 Mary 106
 Nancy 69, 89
 Nancy Jane 106
 Priscilla 106
 Starkey E. 17
 Susan 109
 William 89
Modlin, Margaret 65
 Nathan 74
Mohn, Eli 8
 Sarah 8
Mongomery, Margaret 12
Monk, Linah 56
 Nottingham 7, 71, 100
Montgomery, Elizabeth 75
 Sarah 3
 Wm. 63
Moor, Celia 42
 Josiah 45
Moore, Bitha 70
 Charles S. 89
 Drucilla 49
 Eli 82
 Elizabeth 42
 Epaphras 5
 Jane 77
 John 4, 12, 34, 52, 79, 93, 110
 Joseph 3, 85, 95
 Josiah 38, 89
 Martha 20
 Mary 38
 Maurice 70
 Milley 46
 Penelope 38
 Salley 38
 Sally 83
 Sarah 1, 35
 Shadrach M. 66
 Titus 1
 William Ann 89
 Winnafred 50
More, Deliley 46
 Presila 93
Morgan, Elizabeth 28
 John 23
 Magt. Jane 65
 Mark 103
 Mary 99
 Mazy 28
 Nancy 12
 Penelope 71
 Seth 78
Moring, William 37
 William F. 36
Moriss, John 8
 Zadock 68
Morris, Abraham 33
 Archabald 33
 Caroline 47
 Clarissa 70
 Cloe 2
 Edward 67
 Elizabeth 34
 Henneretta 51
 Jarsey C. 76

124

Morris (cont.)
Joseph 70
Martha 6, 59, 68
Martha Ann 23
Mary 94
Mary F. 6
Sally 32
Winnefred 66
Morriss, Eliza 69
John 66
Joseph 68
Kiddy 78
Malinda 60
Matthew 68
Milley 8
Moses 71
Penelope 108
Pernicia 49
Sarah 66
William 8
Winefred 99
Mosre (?), Joseph 16
Moss, Thos. 80
Mott, Sally 51
Mountain, Patrick H. 62
Mullen, Greenbery 96
Mary 100
Murray, Caroline 88
Lucy 53
Mary 51
Muzell/Mizell, Cinthea 38
Muzells/Mizell, Harriet 16
Myers, Eliza 33
Harriet 11
Martha 33, 51
Nash, Dorcas 31
Nazery, Amelia 87
Newborn, Deborah 95
Thomas 60, 95
Newsom, Joseph 84
Nicholls, Fanny 2
H. 10
Harry 33
Hump. 41
Humphrey 103
Humphry 40
Mary 103
Sally F. 103
W. 28
Wright 32
Nichols, Humphrey 58
Noah 38
Sarah 60
Nicoles (?), Renney 67
Niel, Mary 56
Nixon, Alexander 69
Martha 109
Nobles, Solomon 7
Norfleet, Anarchy 41
Frances E. 100
Jno. 1
Margaret 47
Mary R. 100
Stephen A. 100
Norflet, Absila 7
Mary 35
North, Ann 7
Northcott, Bettie A. 71
Northcut, Annie C. 96
Nowell, Polley 83
Sally 109
Oder, Joseph 69
Wm. 73
Oliver, Andrew 46, 88
John 74
Malachi 84
Sarah 52

Outhouse, Israel 6, 26
Outlaw, Adaline 70
Anne 84, 96
Annie P. 95
Cynthia 38
David 21, 74, 92
Dicey 71
Drissallah 35
Edward, Jr. 74
Elizabeth 64, 69
Elleanor 74
Emiline 77
Ferbe 88
Geo. 12, 18
Geo. B. 34, 45
George 34, 74
H. E. 96
Harriet 23
Jacob 50, 63, 110
Jane E. 85
Janie 2
Jeremiah 78
John L. 85
Joshua 2
Judy C. 78, 97
Kida Elizur 21
Lewis 12, 35
Martha Ann 67, 71
Mary 3, 4
Mary E. 46
May A. 18
Morgan 74
Nancy 56
Patsey 50, 106
Peggy 39
Rachel 21
Rachel E. 34
Ralph 94
Sally 35
Sally Ann 21
Sarah 12
Sarah M. 46
Silyey 110
Victoria 82
Victoria R. 1
William 74, 80
Winnefred 2
Outterbridge, Stephen 2, 102
Overton, Tabithy 107
Wm. 24
Owens, Agatha 75
Delina 75
Oxley, A. 84
Amanda 16
Ann 101
Elizabeth 12
Hardy 64
John 46, 64, 90, 101,
Martha 46
Mary E. 61
Olive 90
Salley 84
Page, James 107
Joshua M. 75
Nancy 17
Nathan 21, 50
Solomon 30, 43
Palmer, Mat B. 24
Matthias B. D. 9
Rebecca 45
Parker, Eleanor M. 46
Elisha 76
Jane 111
John 42
Luke 25, 75, 94
Martha A. 7
Mary 24, 71

Parker (cont.)
Mary Elizer 19
Nancy 94
Reuben 76
Richard 4
Sallie F. 90
Sarah 78
Thena 49
Parnell, Rebecca 86
Parrott, Augustin 36
Patrick, Caroline V. 59
Peal, Betsey 27
Peale, W. M. 80
Pearce, Elisabeth 78
Elizabeth A. 92
Jeremiah 96
Mathew 41, 79
Priscilla 41
Sally 106
Pearson, J. 89
Pedin, Sarah 64
Peeele, James 77
Peel, Aletha 14
William 46
Peele, Adelia 61
Celia 6, 13
Elizabeth 73
Emilla Jane 15
Judah 43
Martha 69
Mary 87
Mary E. 43
Mary F. 12
Ophelia L. 40
Sarah Jane 14
Warren 73
Wm. 20
Peells, Mary 27
Pender, Elisha 58
John 29, 75
Polly 52
Solomon 52, 83
W. 81
Penney, Nancey 6
Perry, Basha 13, 37
Caroline 71
Celia 7
Edith 22
Elizabeth 51
Frances 104
Freeman 78
Friza 9
Harriet 50
Harriet Ann 78, 79
John 54
John, Jr. 24
Kiddy M. 51
Martha 78
Martha A. 51
Martha R. 44
Martin 78
Mary 54
Mary Ann 78
Mary June 39
Nancy 40, 88
Penelope 88
Salley J. 78
Sally Cherry 79
Sarah 84
Temperance 78
Wm. 20
Persey, John 78
Peteman, Henry 12
Peton, Sarah 66
Petty, John 18-
Phelps, Asa 92
Casandra 79
Christian 37

Phelps (cont.)
  Elizabeth 20
  Hary 13, 70
  Mary M. 5
  Penelope C. 37
  Sally 23
  Sarah 107
  Susan A. 79
  Syntha 57
Phillaw, Jinnette 26
Philps, Margaret 16
Phulks, Elizabeth 15
Pierce, Acenith 57
  Anne 76
  David 17
  Elizabeth 11
  Esther 97
  Francis Jane 17
  George Washington 41
  John 105
  Harriet 29
  Margaret J. 79
  Matilda 57
  Penelope 79
  Priscilla 62
  Sarah 54
Pike, Nancy 96
Piland, Lucinda 29
  Sarah A. 29
  Sophia 85
Pilont, Sarah 72
Pinner, Arthur 74
Pirkens, Fanney 72
Pitman (?), Winnefred 42
Pond, Margt. 93
Pool, Rose 59
Powell, Ann 108
  Cader 33
  Celia F. 80
  Daniel 75
  Elizabeth 80
  George 45
  James 3
  Jemima 45
  Luvena 19
  Martha 80
  Martha F. 112
  Mary 45, 74, 86, 112
  Mary E. 65, 88
  Patsey 105
  Richard 112
  Saml. 25
  Sarah 3
  Willis 46, 112
  Wm. 91
Power, Sarah 19
Price, Caroline 16
Pritchard, Abba 48
  Absolom 92
  Anna 47
  Calvin 67
  Christopher 17
  Drew 81
  Harriette 16
  James 23, 81
  John W. 81
  Jonathan 81
  Kezee 17
  Mary 17
  Penaritta 21
  Rachel 49
  Sarah Francis 27
  Sinna 77
  Wm. 53
Pruden, D. 49
  David 49, 82, 98
  Jacob 48
  Lucinda 110

Pruden (cont.)
  Mary 49
  Rebecca 35
  Wm. S. 4, 68
Pugh, Adaline 82
  Amelia 14
  Catharine 10
  Elizabeth C. 82
  Emiline 64
  F., Jr. 33
  Fannie 108
  Frances 73
  Francis 19, 101, 109
  Hinney 84
Pugh (?), Jno. H. 77
Pugh, Laura Slade 109
  Lindona 61
  Margaret 47
  Mary 84, 98
  Mary E. 33
  Penelopy 106
  Sally 17
  Thos. J. 56
  Thos. Whitmell 62
Purvis, Penelope 43
Quall (?), Polly 67
Quinnby, Nanny 106
Raby, Benten H. 43
  Blake D. 86
  Esther 85
  Harriet D. 85
  Henrietta 70
  Sally 82
Raiby, Jannet 100
Rasco, William 85
Rascoe, Lucy 74
  Mary 61
  Mary Ann 82
  Mema 37
  Sarah 20
  Sarah F. 58
  William 44
Raser, Jesse 5
Rasior, Milley 75
Rasor, Edward 63
  Edwd. 39
  Frances 2
  Josiah 18
  Martha 18
Rawles, Elizabeth W. 77
Rawls, Eliza 102
  Jonas 25
  Mary Ann 13
  Mary M. 27
  Wm. 9
Ray, Fanny W. 73
  Henry 95
  James 28
  John 13
  Olive 37
  Patience 75
  Penny 65
  Thomas 83
  William 98
Raybey, Mary 3
Rayner, Amos 9
  Ann E. 76
  Anna E. 14
  Dicy 97
  Elijah 19, 43, 44
  Enock 82
  Mary 83
  Mary A. 33
  Nancy 50
  Octavia 73
  Penelope 60
  Sally 97
Rayser, Mary 62

Razer, Elizabeth 8
  Mary 63
Razor, Isabella 29
Rea, Frances 37
  Macey 86
Reasons, Sarah 94
Reddit, Lewis 55
Redditt, Josiah 41, 112
  Margaret E. 35
  Sarah 64
  Theophilus 56
Reed, E. 46
  Elizabeth 58
  John 52
  Keziah 53
  Leml. S. 81, 102
  Lemuel S. 88
  Mary 88
  Olive 65
Rehlache/Roulhac, Hasty 95
Rhoads, Charles 2
Rhodes, Ann E. 83
  Clara 5
  Elisabeth 61
  Elisha 75
  Elizabeth 86
  Ephraim 27
  Francis 49
  Henry 108
  James 31
  John 69
  John A. 111
  John H. 25
  Lucy 77
  Mary 10, 58
  Milley 96
  N. 26
  Nancy 57, 86
  Nazareth 45
  Penney 70
  Rebecca 51
  Salley 3
  Thomas 87
  Urodilla 50
  William 38, 44, 93
  Winefred 38
  Wm. 20
  Wm. H. 110
Rice, Ann Rebecca 81
  Dorsey 48
  Harriet 44
  Jane 48
  John 48, 71
  John, Jr. 105
  Martha Ann 96
  Priscilla 72
  Sarah F. 97
  Wm. 81
Ricks, M. E. 107
Riddle, Polley 53
Riggsby, William 58
Rigsbey, Anne 19
  Josiah 19
Rigsby, Nancy 26
Roades, Henry 85
Roads, John 85
Roberson, Ann 40
  Martha 3
  Sarah 46
Robertson, Nancy 81
  Sally Francis 13
  Senith 46
Robins, William 89
Robinson, John 35
Rodes, Sarah 96
Rogers, Frederick 28
  Penny 55
  Sarah 28

Ross, James 8
Mary 104
Roulhac, Maria 33
Roundtree, Judeth 1
Rountree, Eliza 108
Rowan, John 82, 86
Ruark, Sarah 110
Ruffin, Ann 86
Bernetta 82
Charlott 91
Frederick 112
John 10
Joseph 3
Mary W. 91
Sally 58
Thos. 9
William J. 46
Runnels, Prudence 107
Russell, David (?) 21
Rutland, Charity 42
Elisabeth 39
Elizabeth 87
James 38
John 44
Norsworthy 39
Watson 87
Whitmell 57
Wm. 26
Rutter, Williamson 55
Ryan, David 58, 87
Emily Turner 38
Gracy 88
Harriet A. 7
James 90
M. C. 103
Marcus C. 87, 90
Martha (Mrs.) 61
Sarah 87
Thomas 87
Sackey, Rachel 68
Sanderlain, Moses 87
Wm. 87
Sanderlin, Mary 53
Sue 85
Sandrum, Will 24
Sarrinn (?), Sarah 41
Savage, Rachel 92
Saward, Margaret 10
Sawell, John 110
Scott, Betsey 26
Seals, Mildred 55
Thomas 28, 55
Seawell, Milley 59
Seay (?), Margaret 1
Sessoms, Jos. W. 111
Nancy Adaline 3
Sharrack, Mary E. 3
Whitmill T. 70
Sharrock, Elisabeth 50
W. T. 70
Shaw, Francis A. 61
John 28
Margaret P. 78
Martha M. 22
Mary 59
Samuel 59
Wm. 93
Shehan, Ann 89
Edward M. 82
Frederick 89
Rachel 112
Thomas 83
Thos. 2
Shields, Mary O. (Mrs.)
13
Sholar, Cader 104
Easter 104
Happy 52

Sholar (cont.)
John 89
Joshua 49
Nancy 11, 89
Ruth 14
Salley 32
Solomon 43
Thomas 34, 84, 101
Shoular, Elizabeth 43
Shoulder, Ephraim 61
Shoulders, Fanny 75
Simmons, Agnes B. 39
Francis A. 46
Jeremiah 84
Lucy A. 73
Mary E. 36
May R. 41
Zd. S. 101
Zebulon 58
Simons, David C. 89
David L. 69
Elizabeth 16, 69
Fanny 38
George 16, 57
Joseph 23
Josephine J. 91
Mollie J. 12
William 75
Simpson, Enoch 71
Siscomb, Sidney 55
Skiles, Jinnet 83
John 13, 24, 58
Jonathan 12
Mary 58
Nancy 30
Starkey 83
Thamer 13
William 62, 94, 110
Wm. 37
Skinner, Phereby 1
Skyles, Sally Ann 99
Slade, Agnes J. 32
Alfreda 40
Amelia 58
John 11, 94
Thomas P. 9
Slatter, Thos. 90
Slaughter, William H. 111
Smallwoood, Edy 91
Emma 90
Louisa 109
Lucy 95
Sarah E. 39
Smith, Ann 23
Anna (Mrs.) 10
Bryan 1, 30
Delilah 70
Elizabeth 40
Fanny 28
Harvy 92
Henry 26
Isaiah 92
James W. 52
Jestenna 104
John 29, 41, 55, 91, 92
Lucy 92
Marina 76
Martha 47
Mourning 41
Nancy 53
Nathan 43
Penelope 71
Pheriby 14
S. B. 76
Salley 84
Senith 98
Stark (Dr.) 68
Stark B. 107

Smith (cont.)
Susanah 28
Teletha 15
Thomas 47
Wfley Ann 4
William 70, 91, 111
Winefred 101
Winney 2
Wm. B. 90
Smithwick, Ann 82
Ebenezer 57
Hum. R. 18
Hypy. 76
John 63, 70, 82
Lanier 93
Luke 6, 29, 39, 83
Margaret A. 47
Martha 29
Sarah 52, 63
William 75, 92, 93
Snow, John 65
South, Andrew 14
Clarissa 79
Mary 92
Samuel 18, 47, 83, 112
Sarah 20
Sowel, Sarah 81
Sowell, Ezekiel 1, 21, 27
James 3
Sowell (?), John 74
Sowell, Mary 70
Nancy 21
Sarah 27, 46
William 97
Winefred 68
Winnefred 1
Wm. 7, 24, 75, 77
Sparkman, Edward 17
Elisabeth 17
Elizabeth 52, 72
George 17, 99
James 93
Jesse 52
Sarah 99
William 60
Winefred 34
Wm. R. 93
Wm. Reed 81
Speight, Lydia 23
Sarah 60
Speights, Winefred 11
Speller, Kary 93
Kary Ann 93
Mary E. 85
Sarah R. 102
Thos. H. 104
Spence, Elisabeth 38
T., Jr. 24
Thomas 69
Thos. 1, 4
Spencer, Susanah 39
Spight, Rachel 37
Spive, Ann 111
Spivey, Aaron 84
David 4
Elisabeth 1
Jonathan 15, 37, 67, 93,
96, 97
Joseph B. 49
Lewis 48
Margt. E. 12
Martha 58
Moses 111
Rachel 22
Sarah E. 15
William 3, 64
Wm. 67
Spivy, Dililah 41

Spruil, Sally 19
Stainback, Sarah 31
Stall, Frances 108
Stallings, Elisabeth 7
  Josiah 74
  Mary 80
  Mary E. 47
  Phillip 7
Standley, Apraley 13
  David 21, 95, 98
  John 15, 66
  Jonathan 84, 93, 94
  Margaret 67
  Martha 74
  Mary 94, 97
  Sarah 4
  William 4
Stanton, Ann 16
  Elizabeth 91
Steely, James B. 85
Stevens, Sarah 86
Stewart, Jennet 50
  John 50, 102
  P. 46
  Sarah 88
  Sarah E. 16
Stokes, Pheby 96
Stone, Ann 47
  Debby 14
  Mary 63
  Sarah 59
  Sparkman 95
  William 89, 101, 104
  Zedh. 51
Strachan, D. 10, 98
Strother, K. T. 10
Stuart, James 7
Sumner, Christen 5
  Elisha 39
Surry, Sarah 93
Sutton, E. T. 26
  Elisabeth 83
  John 92
  Mary 56
  Mildred 83
  Thomas 19, 60, 83
  William 20, 64, 92, 101, 112
Swain, Anna 69
  Elizabeth 30
  Mary A. 98
  Richard 96, 101
  Sarah 101
  Thos. 53
  William 91
Sweatman, James 101
Swinson, Richard 2
Tabert, Pressy 107
Tadlock, Absalom 100, 103
  Ann E. 46
  Martha 101
  Rebecca 53
Tarlington, Seasey 19
Tart, James 74
  Jas. 93
  Nathan 93
  Patsey 74
  Pherby 93
Taylo, Penelope 34
Tayloe, Amanda Jane 106
  Ann 82
  Anne 49
  D. E. 76
  David 70
  Elisabeth 32
  Eveline 102
  Irrha 20
  J. S. 70

Tayloe (cont.)
  James 32, 46
  Jona. S. 7, 9, 18, 22, 39, 50, 56, 63, 67, 81, 82, 85, 86, 110, 111
  Josephine 96
  Lucy 47
  Margaret 100
  Martha Jane 52
  Mary 26
  Richard R. 42
  Robert R. 53
  Robt. R. 81, 85
  Teresa 46
Taylor, Belinda 15
  Elizabeth 31
  Isaac Rebecca 85
  Jane 6
  Martha 67
  Richard 81
  Robt. R. 110
Teal, Thos. 64
Temples, Ann 18
Terry, Lewis D. 85
Thomas, Elizabeth 16
  Ezekial 89
  Hannah 6
  James 74
  John 12, 75
  Jos. 6
  Josiah 94, 98
  Judeth 107
  Judy 34
  Laodicia 89
  Lewis 17
  Martha 35, 39
  Mary 42
  Mikel 6
  Nancy 69
  Rachel Emily 77
  Sarah 12, 33
  Winefred 107
  Winnifred 69
Thompson, A. H. 97
  Amy 8
  Betsey 98
  Christian E. 70
  Clary 107
  David 102
  Eliza 85
  Elizabeth 59, 91
  Harriet 98
  Lucretia 79
  Margaret J. 30
  Mary 7
  Mary A. C. 37
  Mildred 102
  Noah 42
  Phoebe 30
  Rachel 109
  Sarah 22, 80
  Sarah E. 49
Thorowgood, Mary 108
Tinch, Henrietta F. 41
Tiner, Salley 105
  Winefred 15
Toary (?), William 40
Todd, Aquilen 99
  Charlotte 11
  Elisha 40
  Eliza 104
  Francis 65
  Hardy 69, 93
  James 51
  Lamuel 99
  Luis 40
  Martha 65, 66, 69

Todd (cont.)
  Martha Jane 42
  Nancy 83, 90
  Nancy C. 104
  Pernice 54
  Sally 91
  Samuel 83, 98
  Sarah A. 90
  Selah 10
  William 99
  Zilpha 101
Tomlingson, Ebenezer 80
Toole, Jeralden 29
Tucker, James 17
Tunstall, Elisabeth 82
  Lucy 109
Turnage, Huldy Hobbs 62
  William Hobbs 62
Turner, Abishae 90
  Anne 47
  Edward 93
  Elisabeth 36
  Elizabeth 76
  Ellen 21
  Hannah 22
  James 94, 100
  John 35
  Martha 35, 64
  Mary 98
  Pelelope J. 109
  Sarah 70, 96
  Thos. 22
  Thos. Jr. 109
  William 64, 80, 84, 96
  Wm. 24
Twain, Latchworth 51
  Susannah 51
  William 39
Twine, Mary 83
Tyler, C. C. 72
  Drucilla 91
  Elizabeth 43
  Mary 9
  Temperance A. R. 72
Tyner, Amelia 47
  Elisabeth 40
  Temperance 107
Umflet, Job 31
Urquhart, Alexander 57
  R. A. 100
Valentine, Nancy Jane 8
  Sarah E. 30
Vann, Elizabeth 91
  Henry 46
  William 91
Vaughan, Leincestan 51
Veal, Margaret 86
  Richard 86
Veale, Agness 100
  Catherine 39
  E. C. 56
  Elizabeth 5
  Margaret A. 30
  Richd. 39
  Thomas 100
  Venus 73
  W. 4
Ventures, Mary 51
Vinson, Martha 40
Volines, Frances 52
W__(?), Elizabeth 22
Wair, G. 100
  Garrord 12
  George 47, 75
Wair (?), Judah 34
Wall, Thomas 88
Wallace, Mary 110
Waller, Elizabeth 68

Williams (cont.)
Benj. B. 37
Browning 109
Catharine 72
Celia 80
Delylah 36
Dilla 109
Eliza Ann 23
Elizabeth 48, 72
Frances 1
George 20
Harriet 98
Isaac 84
James 49
Jarsey Ann 67
Jno. 105
Jno. B. 103
John 30
John F. 38
Joseph 48
Lisina 108
M. F. 96
Margaret 9
Margret 98
Martha 32, 78, 98
Mary 11, 44, 48, 95
Mary E. 101
Mary Elizabeth 66
Nancy 97
Peny 22
Rebecca Ann 45
Rena Ann 32
Samuel 24
Sarah 13, 45, 66, 84
Susan 45
William 15, 57, 108
Wm. 45
Williford, Abner 50
Adaline 100
Asa 4
Hester 45
James 1, 4, 32
John 67
Martha 67
Martha A. 110
Mary 111
Polley 4
Sarah 32
William 56
Wright 47, 72, 73
Willoughby, John 71
Jos. G. 76
Joseph G. 83
Mary E. 71
Tempy 71
Wilson, Bartra 45
Catherine 50
Edward 107
Elizabeth 17
Isack 17
Jamima 41
Jane 93
Rebecca 20
Tiney 26
Turner 47
Wimberley, Elizabeth 5,
28
John 43
Wimberly, Frederick 111
Penelope 58
Winants, Hetty 89
Winant 28
Winborn, Alfred D. 90,
111
Winbourn, Sarah 82
Winston, P. H. 13
Wolfenden, John 27, 29,
51, 72

Wood, Happy 13
James 17
Jesse 4, 107
Keziah 103
Suesanah 45
William 13, 45, 91
Winefred 8
Wm. 39
Woodard, Sarah E. 58
Worley, Clarisa 58
Daniel 22, 89
Sarah 58
Sarah S. J. 36
Susan L. 9
Thomas M. 104
W. G. 111
Wright, Joseph 22, 94
Wynants, Elizabeth 60
Penelope 56
Wynn, Mary 54
Wynns, Elizabeth 14
G. 111
George 54
John 4, 38
Mary J. 80
Nancy C. 49
William M. D. 101
Wm. McD. 111
Wright 112
Yates, Rhodea 3
Sarah Frances 70
Yearley, Benjamin 42
Elisabeth 72
Yeates, Izreal (?) 50
James 84
Yeats, David 12
Griffen 112
James 105
John 39
Young, Daniel 109
Dolphin Drew 86
Jannett 52
Sarah 59
Thomas 59
Whitson 40
Zellner, George P. 95